CONTENT

A 7 STEP CONTENT MARKETING HANDBOOK:

HOW TO GROW YOUR BUSINESS WITH INSANELY SHAREABLE CONTENT

ANDREW AND PETE

ABOUT THE AUTHORS

Andrew and Pete help solopreneurs and business owners create insanely shareable content that builds brands people love. As international keynote speakers, they have been featured on sites such as Social Media Examiner, Entrepreneur on Fire, Convince and Convert, Kim Garst and Huffington Post. Following the hit book *'The Hippo Campus'*, *'Content Mavericks'* is the second book published by the duo.

Find out more about growing your business with clever marketing at www.andrewandpete.com

For all you inspiring MAVERICKS.

CONTENTS

THE SCENE SETTER

[Mood Music]

Content Marketing is DEAD

Blogging is DEAD

Twitter is DEAD

Facebook organic reach is DEAD

Snapchat is DEAD

Are you as sick as we are with people claiming '*Every way to promote your business* is DEAD'?

You see, the only thing that's DEAD is the old ways of doing things. Just like they've always been.

The old way of doing Content Marketing is DEAD.
The old Twitter strategies are DEAD.
The old ways of getting seen on Facebook are DEAD.

Yet business owners and marketers will forever get their knickers in a twist, because they can't see what is inevitably coming... that what worked last year might not work today.

This is a book about content marketing. Is it as simple to do content marketing these days as it was five years ago? Nope!

Why? Because NEWSFLASH: having a 'blog' isn't novel anymore! Everybody and their dog has a blog.

Does that mean 'blogging is dead'? Again... nope!

It just means that simply 'having a blog' ain't gonna cut it.

You know what will never be dead? ... Innovation.

(OK that was far too cheesy to be the 339th word of this book.)

Let's try that again... do you know what will never be dead? Stand Out Marketing.

Stand out marketing will never be dead because it looks at what's *different* and focusses on that. As soon as what's different becomes the norm, stand out marketing changes to suit. It always asks... what's different now? How do we get attention TODAY? Why doesn't this work anymore?

This is a book about content marketing. But more specifically it's a book about how to execute content marketing in a stand out way. We've got seven modules for you to go through, and you should really read them in order as each one builds upon the next.

The end goal is to give you a process of how to do content marketing in a *maverick* way - that's going to get you noticed and generate sales. Along the way we tackle topics like:

- Why the hell are you doing this?
- What the hell are you going to create?
- Why are you so goddamn boring?
- How the **** are you going to organise all this?
- Where's my reach at bro?

& ...

- So, when do I make money with this again?

There are more bits in between, but we didn't want to overwhelm you... YET ;)

P.S. One final thing... sometimes we forget not everybody knows this... but there's two of us. Andrew and Pete. It's a dual-authorship kind of thing. Imagine two people reading out this book in unison if it helps.

P.P.S. This is the only reference to Top Gun in the WHOLE book.

Enjoy the read!

Go forth, and be a Content Maverick.

MODULE 1:
CONTENT MINDSET

So you think of a blog...

You start researching the blog...

You start writing the blog...

You get distracted on Facebook... (happens to the best of us!)

You finish writing the blog...

You add images to the blog...

You proof the blog...

You publish the blog...

You have a celebratory beverage... (you deserve it!)

You promote the goddamn blog...

You've put all this time and effort into this blog, you've

promoted it your audience, you're all excited and what happens...?!

NOTHING!

Nada, zero, zilch...

No likes, no comments, no shares, definitely no sales, just silence... crickets in the distance chirping... mocking you...

There's nothing worse than putting all that time and energy in creating a piece of content and getting nothing back.

We call these 'Content Crickets', and they suck! It's hard to keep on going when there seems to be no foreseeable return on your blood, sweat and tears.

We hear all the time that "content marketing is hard", and you know what... it can be. But it can also be fun, rewarding and generate a boat-load of business too!

The first step, though, is having the right mindset. When we talk about mindset, this isn't a light and fluffy starting point. We want you to read this section carefully, because although we're laying down some foundations and principles of content marketing, we're also going to teach you some cool stuff that will switch up your thinking.

During this section, we're going to get you thinking about what types of content you should *really* be creating, what content is appropriate, depending on how well the reader knows you, and when it's right to use salesy messages.

We're also going to tell you what most people do wrong when they start out, so you don't do the same.

Let's jump in!

WHAT IS CONTENT MARKETING?

The following definition comes from the founding fathers of content marketing - The Content Marketing Institute:

"Content marketing is a strategic marketing approach, focussed on creating and distributing valuable, relevant and consistent content to attract and retain a clearly defined audience, and ultimately, to drive profitable customer action."

...phew...

This is a great explanation of content marketing, although it can seem long-winded and overwhelming when you're new to the idea.

In simple terms, we want to create content that makes people feel **happier or smarter** to build an audience and turn that audience into sales.

Why Trust and Attention are Killing Businesses

There's a direct correlation between how much attention and trust you have, and how much money you'll make. In this day and age, the internet has completely revolutionised the game. With an influx of new competitors and with consumers having a wealth of information at their fingertips, *attention* and *trust* are at an all-time low.

TRUST IS AT A LOW. There are so many charlatans in all industries who are destroying trust to the point where it isn't there anymore. It's hard to know who to buy from online; they may look professional, but you can't tell who knows what they're doing and even worse - what's just a scam.

ATTENTION IS AT A LOW. Think of all the distractions we have in the world. People aren't focussed on one medium at a time anymore. They may be checking their email, watching TV on their iPad, WhatsApping their bestie, eating a bagel and feeding the cat, all at the same time as being on the phone using their Apple Watch!

People's attention is now split. We can't command the same attention we once could by doing what we've always done.

The Antidote

The Content Mavericks Model is the perfect antidote to this. Creating content that makes people feel **happier or smarter** is the perfect way to grab attention (who doesn't want to be happier or smarter?!), and an even more perfect way of developing trust with your audience over time, by showing them (not telling them) how awesome you really are.

DEVELOPING BRAND EQUITY

A great way to describe how this all works is by using Ryan Deiss' *Equity Model,* which compares content marketing to a bank.

BUILD EQUITY

The way banks work is simple: you put in money - build some equity over time - then withdraw money when you want to buy a new pair of shoes.

(Who said you would just learn about content marketing with this book?)

**BUILD BRAND
EQUITY**

Content marketing works in exactly the same way. You publish content for your audience, which over time builds your 'brand equity'. The more consistently amazing content you publish, the more your brand equity grows and therefore the more sales you can 'withdraw'.

We love the analogy of building 'brand equity'. Sure, we can't necessarily measure exactly how much equity we have with each member of our 'audience', but we can imagine that every time we make somebody feel happier or smarter, our equity builds. We're earning the right to withdraw sales.

This is why you have to get consistent with content. One blog 'every now and then' doesn't build all that much equity!

Does That Mean This is a Long-Term Strategy?

Good question! *(Yes, we know we asked that one ourselves.)*

Marketers bang on all the time about content marketing being a long-term strategy, don't they?

We think that is bloody annoying to be frank. Because what good is that?!?! We need to eat this month, pay our rent this month, feed our fish this month, buy Beyoncé's new album today.

So what good is having a 'long term-marketing strategy'? It's bonkers.

Here's our angle on this...

Content marketing is a long-term strategy, that has short term gains if executed well.

So yes, it's a long-term strategy in that the more consistently we do this over time, the more brand equity we will build and the more withdrawals of sales we'll be able to take.

However, if you're a start-up and need this to work in the short-term - it will... if executed correctly.

If you follow the process in this book, you'll be creating content in a different way to your competitors, that gets you noticed by the right people in the short term. You'll be doing things differently, making your mark and building brand equity extremely quickly to generate short-term sales. You'll be a Content Maverick.

But what if you're an existing business? That's cool too. You have a bit of a head-start because you probably already have some kind of audience or awareness.

In fact, that was us. We set up shop in 2011, but it took us a good few years to understand this process, and map out what worked.

We were blogging for years and not really getting much from it, but the moment we upped our game with our content in a remarkable way, things started to blow up. We saw immediate short-term sales, as our audience members who weren't really that interested previously were switched on to what we're all about. We made our cold connections feel **happier and smarter**.

Nowadays, we find it interesting how brand equity builds differently for different people. Some people may come across our content and KNOW we are a good fit for them immediately, and sometimes it can take a few months, or even years for them to buy. Later on in this module we'll show you how and why it's important to nurture the people who aren't ready to buy yet.

BY-PRODUCTS OF CONTENT MARKETING

So you can probably tell by now we are super-passionate about content marketing. We know how it generates sales, but through this process WHAT ELSE are you going to get?

Audience-Building: The bigger your audience, the more potential people there are to buy from you. BUT, you can't build an audience if you've got nothing to say! If you want to build your audience, you need to produce valuable, engaging and interesting content that makes people feel **happier or smarter** (yep, those two words again).

Authority: As you create content, people will look up to you as an expert in your field. And with authority comes power (insert evil laugh here). Your lead time is shortened, you can charge more, you'll be invited to collaborate, you'll get speaking gigs, your web traffic will go up, your ego will inflate and every 'authority' in the world gets free popcorn at the cinema... fact!

SEO and Archives: This isn't a book about Search Engine Optimisation (nor do we profess to be SEO aficionados), but this book will have a direct positive benefit on your SEO results. Creating content means your domain authority will build, you will start to rank more, get more traffic, more links, more internal linking opportunities and more other good stuff the SEO experts will tell you about.

Scalability: Scalability in content marketing means you can reach an unlimited number of potential customers. One bit of content could live forever and ever and keep converting customers forevermore. We used to do a ton of in-person networking, but we could only meet a certain number of people and once the event was over that was it. We started investing our networking time into 'content creation', so we can reach people in a scalable way and as regularly as we decide. [Side note: We do still see the value in face-to-face networking, but think people rely too much on it rather than thinking bigger].

Credibility: So you may not want to be an authority but do you want to appear 'credible'? We'd guess so. Content leads to credibility, as you are showing - not telling - what you know. In our early 20s (when we looked about 13) we had to *show* people we knew what we were talking about - we couldn't do that without content.

Upskilling: This isn't an obvious benefit of content marketing, but we've found that consistently producing content pushes us to learn more and keep on the cutting edge. Everybody knows that they need to upskill themselves, learn new stuff and keep up with the latest trends in their industry, but how many people are proactively doing that? Tie content marketing into your marketing plan and you'll kill two birds with one stone.

ANDREW AND PETE'S CONTENT MODEL

We created Andrew and Pete's Content Model to explain exactly how creating content leads to sales and business growth.

In the model, there are two specific types of content, and it is very important to understand the differences between them.

Primary Rich Content is content that is intended to draw people in and make them feel **happier or smarter**. You're not selling your stuff through your primary rich content - it simply needs to be educational or entertaining to build your brand equity. It is purely there to draw people into your content funnel and grow your audience. This content needs to be 'rich' too. It needs to have some meat to it! For example, a blog, video channel or podcast are all great examples of 'rich' media.

Secondary Conversion Content is content that is designed to generate sales. It's all about what you do, how you do it, and why people should spend money with your business. They may feel **happier or smarter** after consuming this type of content, but the purpose is completely different.

So, let's look at how each of these fits into the model.

Traffic Source

At the very top of the model you start with a traffic source - you need to drive people to your content in some way. The three main ways are social media, SEO and email marketing (more on that in Module 6), but there are countless ways you could be driving traffic to your content.

Primary Rich Content and Share Loop

Importantly, you're driving people to your primary rich content first. You need to win their attention and trust before anything else, and you do that through this type of content.

The great thing about primary content is that it should be highly shareable, thus sending even more traffic back to your content every time someone shares. We call this the Share Loop.

Inspire Action and Subscriber Loop

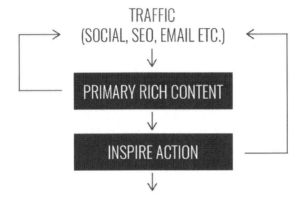

Once they have consumed your primary rich content, you want them to take some kind of action to build more brand equity. You want them to keep consuming your content, as you know more brand equity is built up with each bit of content they consume. It's great to get them reading/listening/watching more of your content, but you also want the power to keep in touch time and time again, so you need them to subscribe to your content: e.g. subscribe to you on YouTube, Like your Facebook Page, join your newsletter.

Subscribing to receive more of your primary rich

content means you can keep in touch and continuously build more and more equity - this is called the Subscriber Loop.

Secondary Conversion Content

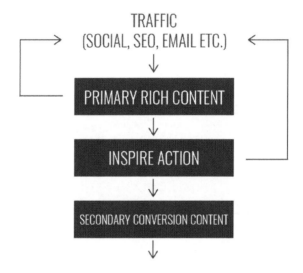

Once the brand equity is built, you should serve the secondary conversion content. The purpose of this is to convert those in your audience who are ready to buy into sales. Due to the subscriber loop, people may have consumed a ton of your content before they are ready to buy. Secondary conversion content is therefore important to allow these people to find out more when they *are* ready.

In Module 7, we talk about exactly how to serve this secondary conversion content to the right people at the right time.

Leads and Sales

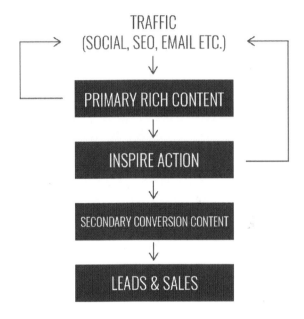

Finally, out of the bottom pops leads and sales!

WHAT TYPE OF CONTENT ARE YOU CREATING?

It's important now to understand what type of content you have been creating up until this point. Have you been creating primary rich content that makes people feel **happier or smarter**? Or have you been creating just secondary conversion content?

We find that most people who have started with content marketing jump straight to the secondary conversion content, because it is easier. You know exactly how to create content like:

- 3 Ways to Use My Product
- Why My Product is the Best in the Business
- 7 Ways to Do Something (Using my product is number 3 BTW)
- A Case Study: On My Product
- The Story of My Product - A Reflective Look Back

But see the problem here? Secondary conversion content is ALL. ABOUT. YOU.

And what if somebody right now just doesn't care about you? What if they aren't ready to buy right now? They're just going to find what you have to say...

- Irrelevant
- Boring

or even worse....

- Downright SPAM

By creating primary rich content, you start building relationships with potential future customers, making them like you and fall in love with you. This gives your marketing effort legs, and makes the returns exponential.

Also, please don't try pass off secondary conversion content as primary rich content. We see people do this ALL THE TIME, and it just cheapens your message.

It's so obvious - everyone knows the intention of your blog isn't to be helpful but to sell your stuff... so don't do it! Yes, we are in marketing, and the purpose of course is to sell more stuff, but your content will have much more impact if you separate it into primary and secondary and give each piece the right intention.

HOW TO CREATE PRIMARY RICH CONTENT

In Module 3 we delve deep into what you need to do to create outstandingly remarkable primary rich content, but for now we just want to get the gears turning.

Primary rich content is developed from understanding people's problems. Because although somebody may not be in the market to buy your product right now, problems are universal:

- I may not want to buy a new exercise bike right now, but I want my favourite shirt to fit better
- I may not want to buy into a de-stressing coaching programme, but I want to be able to chill the f**k out at work
- I may not want to buy a trip to Disneyland with the kids, but I want to know more ways to keep them entertained in the car

See the difference? Start now, by thinking about the potential PROBLEMS your customers have that you can solve with your content.

Are You Content Rich or Content Poor?

The final thing we want you to decide on in this module is if you are Content Rich or Content Poor, as both have challenges to overcome that you need to start thinking about.

Content Rich Industries are the industries where people actually care about what you do, and are interested in finding out about how you do it. Take 'marketing' for example - people want to know how we do what we do, so all we have to do in that industry is talk about marketing your business. Easy, right?!

Well yes, in a way it is easier to think of content ideas, BUT the challenge for a content rich industry is overcrowding. Most content rich industries are full of people creating content, letting you in on the 'secrets', showing you 'how it's done in 10 easy steps'. If you're in a content rich industry too, then your challenge is not WHAT to talk about, but HOW you differentiate yourself from everyone else's content. If you are producing similar content to everybody else, you're just going to be adding to the noise and banging your head against the wall.

Other examples of content rich industries are things like fitness, fashion, personal development, etc. Anything where you can easily create content based on what you do, and there are people who want to consume it.

Content Poor Industries on the other hand, are industries where people don't really care about how you do what you do, but just need or want the outcome. So if you start creating primary content around how you do what you do, you'll see less engagement.

Good examples of this might be things like 'graphic design' or 'copywriting' or even 'funeral directors'.

People don't necessarily care about how you do those things, they just want the outcome... 'an amazing looking logo', 'a kick-ass blog', 'a funeral planned.'

The content you can create may be interesting e.g. "why your logo needs to be a vector", but if you look at your audience (in this case 'business owners'), they don't really need to know that, and you aren't really making them smarter in a way that matters to them. If anything, this content is more useful for upcoming competition in your industry.

Your challenge if you are content poor is to really dig deep as to what your potential customers want to know about, and create content on that.

- I may not need a new logo, but I do want to look amazing online

CREATING YOUR CONTENT MISSION STATEMENT

The final thing we want you to do as part of Module 1 is to create your Content Mission Statement for your primary rich content. You are going to be adding to this as we go, but all we want you to do is fill in the blanks...

I'm going to create content for _____, so they can _____.

In the first gap fill in WHO you are going to create content for, and in the second gap fill in WHAT your content is going to help them with.

Here are some examples:

"I'm going to create content for <u>small business owners</u> so they can <u>feel more confident at work."</u>

"I'm going to create content for <u>women in business</u> so they can <u>have more fun marketing."</u>

"I'm going to create content for <u>car owners</u> so they can <u>keep their car looking great and working well."</u>

"I'm going to create content for <u>people in 9-5 jobs</u> so they can <u>have more fun at the weekend."</u>

Your go!

KEY TAKEAWAYS FROM MODULE 1: CONTENT MINDSET

The main takeaway here is that although content marketing is a long-term strategy, you will get short-term gains if done correctly.

- Primary rich content and secondary conversion content are two distinct content types and should be treated separately for the best results
- Primary content draws people in, and gets them to subscribe for more of your awesome brand equity building content. Secondary conversion content is there to turn this audience into sales
- To create primary content, you really need to understand what PROBLEMS your potential customers have, and how you can help solve those problems, whilst also understanding if you are content rich or content poor

In the next module, we look at Content Branding to give you a strong basis for creating on-brand content that is uniquely YOU.

MODULE 2:

CONTENT BRANDING

Branding is so, so, so important for businesses, and it's something we're extremely passionate about, but it's also the step that almost everyone skims over!

Why is branding so important? Because purchasing decisions have been found to be a mere 20% based on logic, and a whopping 80% based on emotion. Which is crazy if you think about it - 80% of the reason why your clients chose you was because it 'felt' right, because you looked the part, and because you moved them. Not because they thought your service was particularly better than everyone else's!

We actually think it's the missing ingredient for most solopreneurs and small businesses trying to compete in a noisy world. If you don't have a brand that stands out in an overcrowded marketplace, you're going to really struggle.

How do you differentiate yourself? How is your content or the way you work different to your competition? Why should you be someone's favourite? The answers to these questions are all down to the brand. In this day and age, trust and attention are the two most important digital assets, and you can start to achieve both with a remarkable brand. Trust is built from a consistent, positively portrayed image, and being unique through a remarkable brand allows you to cut through the noise and get attention.

If your brand doesn't resonate with your target audience then you will fail.

We're going to show you how to create a remarkable brand for your company that will attract your perfect clients, get them talking about you and buying from you.

Most importantly though, your brand also gives you a framework for coming up with unique content ideas that will enable you to stand out amongst the vast sea of content out there.

The ultimate goal of your content is to instantly set you apart from others, compel your audience to keep consuming, to come back repeatedly, and tell others about you. And let's face it, if your content is vanilla - that just ain't going to happen.

If your content isn't unique, if it isn't building your brand, if it isn't making people fall in love with you, then you're going to have a long, tough journey.

We don't know about you, but we'd much rather spend some time nailing our brand and our content now, than spend the next ten years creating boring content and not getting anywhere. You're wasting your time.

In the next module, *Content Stamp*, we've outlined a process to help you nail down what unique content you can produce, but it all hinges on your brand, so that's why this step is important. Let's work through this together and create your remarkable brand.

WHAT IS A BRAND?

Most people think that a 'brand' refers to aesthetics, such as colours, logos and certain graphic elements. However, that's not what we want to focus on in this module.

Aesthetics are important, but they're not the be-all and end-all. We're not going to talk about how to design something in a certain way, because you need to know *why* that matters to your brand first.

A 'brand' is the gut feeling that people get when working with you. Take a moment to let that sink in. More specifically for our topic, the gut feeling people get when consuming your content.

With ATOMIC, our membership site, people join because they expect to learn something that will enable them to grow their business. But there are lots of other marketing sites out there promising the same thing. The reason they chose to buy from *us* is because they resonate with our brand. It's emotional: they don't want to be alone while they try to improve, they want someone supportive, they want to have fun while they learn, they believe we know what we're on about and because we've been consistent with our content they feel like they can rely on us.

It might have been logic that dictated that they needed to learn more about marketing, but it wasn't logic that made them choose ATOMIC. This is what a good brand does – it makes people *feel* like they want to work with you instantly.

Where most businesses go wrong is that they try to please everyone by being vanilla and putting up this overly professional front.

A lot of start-ups do this almost to overcompensate for their feeling of lack of experience or confidence and we get that - heck, we did it ourselves. We wore suits, used impressive stock photography and had a really professional (boring) looking website. These days we have Andrew being slapped in the face on our homepage! How things change!

While it might seem like a good idea to try to please everyone at first, the only real impact it has is to lose 80% of its potential to draw people in - the emotion.

Imagine having a room of one hundred people. We'd much rather have 50% of that audience avoid us and the other 50% absolutely love us, tell everyone about us and buy all of our products... rather than 100% of the room just look over us and forget about us tomorrow...

What effect would you rather your brand has?

By allowing more of yourself and your company values into your brand and displaying them throughout everything you do, the quicker this will work to resonate and attract the type of clients/customers you want to work with - and repel the rest.

What's more is that the moment you work out your brand, your content will start to excite you (extremely important) and your target market so much more. Your content, once it reflects your brand, will start to work much more powerfully to entice customers, draw them in and make them fall in love with you.

In this day and age, it's no longer good enough for people to just like you, you need to be their favourite!

How do You Evoke a Gut Feeling?

This is so important, and the main focus of this module. We're going to concentrate on five areas: your Brand Values, your Mission, your Avatar, your Arch Enemy and your Lingo. These are the core foundations of a strong brand, and they are going to make your life so much easier once you've nailed them down and applied them.

We talk about brand values a lot with our clients, and we want to challenge anyone reading this book who doesn't have a clear set of their own to create them with us now. It's also a good opportunity to reassess your values if you do have them already.

A brand is essentially what people say about you when you're not in the room. This means you can NEVER control your brand, because after all it's what others *think* and *feel* it is, not what you *say* it is.

It's tough to accept that you can never truly control your own brand, BUT ... you can *influence* it, with consistent messaging across all communications. That's what brand values are - your guidelines for consistency.

If you can consistently get across what you're all about, then eventually people will follow suit.

Here's the test for those of you who know us. Think of three words/phrases that would describe us, Andrew and Pete. Do it now in your head.

What did you come up with? When we ask people this question, no joke, they ALWAYS say something like, "You do things differently to others - you like to stand out, there's two of you and you look like you're always enjoying yourselves - I feel like I'm part of your friendship, but despite the fun you always deliver really practical advice that's really helpful..." Did you come up with something similar?

Well, guess what our brand values actually are:

1. **Rule Breakers** - We don't want to do the same as everybody else in our industry has already done. We want to be innovative, break some rules and make an impact. To be different means you can make a difference.

2. **Besties** - We're best friends and we want that to come across by having fun, but we also want to be friends with you too on this journey with us. We want you to feel like you know us, and we're open.

3. **Inspire Action** - To always enable any skill level to be able to achieve the results they want with practical and motivating training and advice.

Their guesses are pretty much spot on, right? The only reason why people can always do this is because we have nailed our brand values and consistently reflect their message across all our communications.

This is what we want you to do now, decide on your three Stand Out Brand Values that make you unique.

Brand values are all about how you want people to perceive you. If YOU aren't clear about that - how can anyone else be?

NAILING YOUR BRAND VALUES

Here's a good exercise you can do straight away to help you think about your values. Take a sheet of paper or use a whiteboard, and write down all the ways that you'd like to be described when you're not in the room. There are no wrong answers to this!

Write down as many words as you can; you want at least 30. If there's a word that pops into your head that you're not sure applies to you, write it down anyway so you can move on to thinking of more words. You can cross them out later on.

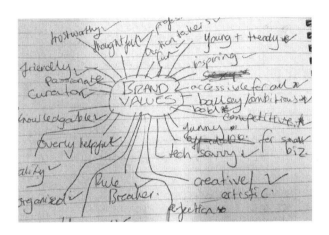

The aim of the exercise is to write down as many as you can. If you're struggling, get a friend to help you, and ask yourself probing questions like:

- How would you like to be described when you're not in the room?
- What makes you different from your competitors?
- What part of your role do you love doing the most?

- What's the most rewarding feeling you give to others?
- What qualities are you most proud of?
- What do others often say you're really good at?
- What has got you furthest in your career?

Eliminate Baseline Values

The next step is to get rid of the industry-specific Baseline Values. These are the values that EVERYONE says in your industry... it's usually something like, 'Quality Service', 'Friendly', 'Professional'... did you write them too? ;)

We call them baseline values because they are still important to have - of course you should be professional and friendly - but they aren't unique and they won't stand out. If you are trying to create a remarkable brand that stands out in your industry, you cannot do that if you base your values on the same things as everyone else, right?!

This means eliminating any values that others in your industry are also likely to say about themselves. These will naturally differ across industries. For example, a marketing company is likely to say:

- Creative
- Friendly
- Knowledgeable

No marketing company would say they *weren't* knowledgeable or creative. If they did, it would be bad business - but it's not going to help them to stand out in the marketing industry if that's *all* they said about themselves. Let's look at some values accountants might use:

- Organised
- Experienced
- Good with numbers

The same thing applies; you expect accountants to be all those things, but 'creative' on the other hand isn't necessarily the word you associate with accountants. So that could be a great stand out value to use and play on.

Go back to your list, and cross out every word that's an industry-specific baseline value. If you've crossed off everything on your paper, you haven't thought hard enough!

Working out Your Overarching Stand Out Brand Values

Now it's time to group the remaining brand values together into three distinctive streams. The idea is to end up with three stand out brand values. Typically, if you start to group the remaining values you've jotted down, they can ALWAYS be grouped together with similar words into three distinctive categories. For example, 'Different', 'Stand Out' and 'Impatient' became for us, 'Rule Breakers'.

Draw out a little table 2 x 3 like below and one by one add your words to it. If a word is in a similar vein as word already in the table, add it to that same row. If it's not a similar word, place it in the next row. Keep doing this until you have all your values grouped into three rows.

Risky, different, pushing boundaries, unexpected, fun, fearless
Practical advice, small business advocates, knows small business troubles, understanding, inspiring, action takers
Feels like I know them, lets me in, open, very friendly, caring, fun to be around, always having fun

The temptation is to allow for four or five brand values because you just can't whittle it down enough. Doing this is no good, as your brand becomes diluted and pulled in too many directions. Plus, you'll never remember five values! If you find yourself stuck and unable to narrow it down to three, then you need to be a little bit harsher with stripping back on the baseline values to find out what really makes you unique.

Once you've got everything grouped into similar areas, you need to give them a stand out headline value, an overarching description that's easy to remember e.g.

RULE BREAKERS	Risky, different, pushing boundaries, unexpected, fun, fearless
INSPIRES ACTION	Practical advice, small business advocates, knows small business troubles, understanding, inspiring, action takers
BESTIES	Feels like I know them, lets me in, open, very friendly, caring, fun to be around, always having fun

Once you have them, you can apply your values to everything you do. Remember these values are for internal use only - you never have to say them out loud in public like we just did (in our defence - one of our values is *Rule Breakers* ;))

Your values should be honest, and something you can relate to. We're not coming up with them to put in our mission statement, or anything like that. YOU have to understand what they mean. Some of our favourite ones, which people have told us, include things like:

- Professional Labrador
- Not a d**khead developer
- Outrageous ambition
- Glass ceiling smasher
- Un-techie
- Prophetic
- Determination of a Rottweiler
- Cheerleader
- Geri Halliwell wannabe

See how these may mean nothing to you, but to the business that has these values, the meaning is super strong to them, and they know how to get that meaning across.

Values can also be used to help you make decisions and come up with new ideas. Below are recent examples from our own business, so you can see how we've applied them to decision making and various communications across 'Andrew and Pete'.

Announcements

Back in early 2016 when we were first asked to speak at Social Media Marketing World 2017 in San Diego, we were incredibly excited and wanted to announce that we were speaking on this huge stage.

Immediately we started to write an email to announce it like you may expect... 'hey check us out, come see us speak at...aren't we amazing...' blah blah blah.

But do you see what's wrong here? We weren't being 'besties' to our audience. When we got the news - as besties together - we went mental: high fives, hugs and drinks all around! So we needed to do the same with our audience - the tone was completely changed to show how excited and humbled we were, and it almost felt like a text to our best friend.

We wanted everyone to feel as excited as us and feel like they were on this journey with us. We didn't want to make people feel that we thought we were better than them for speaking at an international conference, because that's not what your best friend would do.

Speaking at the conference was a huge goal of ours, but by incorporating 'Inspire Action' and 'Rule Breakers', we talked about how we did it and how others could do the same. We talked about our 'domino theory' and about smashing goals.

The response was overwhelming: so many people congratulating us, being excited for us, telling us we deserved it and so on. It really brought out everyone who had played a part in our journey and seen us grow from strength to strength.

Our brand values are who we are and who we always aspire to be, so having them written down often acts as the guidelines necessary to keep us (and you) in line.

While expressing our brand values through our actions is still deliberate, we do it subconsciously a lot more these days, because we've got so used to thinking about how to get the rule-breaking, friendly and inspiring aspects across to our audience.

Branded Photos

We had some new headshot photos taken towards the end of 2016 by Laura Pearman, an amazing photographer. The idea was to top the previous ones she did, which showed us looking like we'd been blown up. We went back to our brand values, and decided to be best friends taking epic selfies together atop a skyscraper.

The resulting photos showed our friendship, our rule-breaking nature, and that if you put your mind to it, you can achieve great heights.

YouTube Channel

Finally, when we started producing videos, we had our three brand values in mind. We knew our videos had to be fun, super engaging and get across some banter between us, but we wanted people to feel like they were having fun with us as well as learning something they could actually take action on.

What Happens Next?

So, what happens once you focus down your unique brand values and all your touch points (every place your customers or potential customers come into contact with you) start to reflect your values? Those gut feelings people have become the words they use to describe you when you're not in the room.

Take the time now to go through this branding exercise and narrow down your three brand values.

YOUR MISSION

Although this can be easier for some companies than others, everyone should be able to come up with a 'mission': why you're in business (other than making cold, hard cash). People can't love a business which is only interested in making money.

Simon Sinek talks a lot about this. He talks about the Power of the Why and the Golden Circle – check him out online for full information. He also came up with the following, which is a great quote:

"Working hard for something we don't care about is called stress. Working hard for something we love is called passion."

This is what we all need to aim towards. We want to feel inspired and creative, so we need to have a passion and a reason for why we do what we do. It doesn't have to be too deep with a 'bigger meaning'; it can just be something that people aspire to in some way. Give people a reason to believe in you and they can, and will, support you forever.

For example, "Reduce poverty" is a great mission, as is, "Have more fun at the weekend", "Help people feel healthier" and even "Help people keep up to date with

Kim Kardashian"! Whatever you come up with, it'll really help you with your business and your 'why'.

For us, we believe that solopreneurs and small businesses have the power to quickly take advantage of new trends and do amazing things ahead of bigger companies, because innovation within bigger companies is often stifled by bureaucracy. Solopreneurs can more readily make quick changes and really push the limits. Often though, they lack the motivation or knowledge to empower themselves - this is where we come in.

Moreover, this motivation to keep learning should be something they like to do, rather than a hassle, otherwise they will never learn as much as they could. We want to enable solopreneurs and small businesses to achieve more than they ever thought possible, via content that empowers them and is delivered in a fun/light-hearted way that they can enjoy watching. This is why we do what we do.

Now let's look back at your content mission statement and add to it:

I'm going to create content for _____ so that they can _____, because
_____.

For instance: "We're going to create content for *solopreneurs* so they can *have more fun marketing* because *we want people to enjoy entrepreneurship and do more than they ever thought possible.*"

Having this statement will, in turn, make it easier to create content that fits with your brand values and resonate with your audience.

YOUR AVATAR

Your Avatar is the ideal customer you want to serve. You need to get specific about who that is, and don't worry about alienating people. Some people love the singer Taylor Swift, but others really hate her. As she says: "Haters Gonna Hate". It doesn't matter what they think, because either way, she's being talked about.

Remember, we'd rather have 50 people love us, and 50 people hate us, than 100 people be indifferent towards us.

You don't want to have a vanilla brand, so you need to focus on who your avatar is and who you're helping with your mission. People worry that by targeting one type of customer nobody else will buy from them, but that isn't the case.

Lots of people who don't fit your avatar **exactly** will still buy from you, as chances are they resonate with your avatar's problems or situation in some way.

To What Level of Detail Should You Know Your Avatar?

The more you know the better! Durrr! ;)

Starting with the basics, you need to know some key demographics such as: gender, location, where they hang out online, job title, hobbies & interests, income, age.

These things are important to know when you're creating your content and marketing messages because it's important to know who you're trying to appeal to. It's also essential information in advert creation when you specify who you want to target.

A lot of this can be filled in from your own gut instincts and experience, but it's always best to use as much data insight, analytics and research as possible.

The major thing you want to know is your avatar's problems. It's those problems they'll be Googling to find the answer to, it's answers to their problems that will draw them in on a busy social timeline and it's answering their problems that will ultimately make them like you at first.

ARCH ENEMY

This is our arch enemy:

He's a suit-douche! Yeh that's a term!

He always wears a full suit and tries to put up this incredibly professional appearance, even though he probably works from home in his pants. He puts you down when speaking to you whilst bragging about clients and making a ton of money. He's overly salesy and slimy, he doesn't care about his customers, only about making more money. He's got no idea about how social media should be used to build meaningful relationships and he's probably partial to a flyer or two!!

In other words, we can't stand him; he's the very opposite of who we want to be.

Having an arch enemy helps you to define who you're not and acts as a guideline to how you should and shouldn't behave, so now we want you to define your own arch enemy.

Now this person doesn't have to actually exist, they can be a combination of many different people, as ours is, but they could be a real person if you have someone in mind.

Here's the thing: your brand values give you something to aspire to, and your arch enemy gives you things to avoid!

When you're thinking of new ideas, campaigns, events and content, ask yourself, "Would my arch enemy do this?" If yes, try to align it more to your values instead.

Look at the opposing brand values to your own, and use these to create your arch enemy. If your values are 'ambitious', 'stylish', 'customer delight', what are the opposites to these? 'Stagnant and samey', 'old-fashioned', 'does the minimum he/she can get away with'.

The brand values don't have to be negative words, though. You could have 'neutral' as the opposite of 'stylish' and 'follows the rules' instead of 'creative.' Choose values that you want to avoid.

It's crazy how many people we've spoken to who've tried marketing techniques/campaigns that haven't worked. When we look at their brand values, they're the exact opposite of the actions they took. It blows people away when they go through this process, because they start to understand why the project they've just completed wasn't on brand and didn't resonate with their audience.

YOUR LINGO

This is how you say stuff! Whether it's written, audio or video, it's about the words you choose to communicate your messages. It's important for content marketing, because it's how you define your 'voice'. It's just one of the ways that you can start to get across your brand values and make sure EVERYTHING is consistently aligned with them.

So, how do you come up with your lingo? First, come up with three voice characteristics that complement your brand values. For example, if your brand values are:

'young and passionate', 'creativity', 'supporting women', you need three characteristics for these.

You don't need an adjective that correlates to each value, just words that express the ideas. Such as: 'informal, quirky, funny', so your content will demonstrate these characteristics for you. If this person was producing a podcast, you'd want the listeners to say: "Check out X's podcast. It's really funny, a bit out there and quirky. It's relaxed and informal, but you actually learn things and X is passionate and creative. She wants to support women, but in an empowering rather than cheesy way."

Write down your characteristics, and look at each of them in turn.

For 'informal', you could, for example, create content in a tone of voice which resembles speech and use formatting for emphasis if you're doing a lot of blogging, such as all caps and bold sentences.

You could create some branded words to show your quirky side. You could tell jokes, poke fun at yourself and be self-deprecating to show your funny side.

Once that's clear, you also need to think about what to avoid. If you're trying to be informal, you don't want to use jargon, long sentences and too much 'fluff.' For quirky, don't use long paragraphs, black and white or 'sensible' content and avoid taking yourself too seriously.

Create your own *Voice Characteristics Table* like this to summarise:

CHARAC-TERISTIC	HOW TO GET THIS ACROSS	WHAT TO AVOID
INFORMAL	Create content in a speech-like tone of voice, use formatting to add emphasis	Jargon, long sentences, being fluffy
QUIRKY	Create some branded words and terms to explain what we do	Long paragraphs, black and white, boring and sensible content all the time
FUNNY	Include jokes, poke fun at ourselves, be a bit self-deprecating	Taking ourselves too seriously

A stellar example of a business which has done this brilliantly is Uberflip, who have a branding and style guide which is available for the public to view: styleguide.uberflip.com

Within it, they have their mission statement, branding, tone of voice and so on, and is a great example of how to go into plenty of detail for your own business.

They describe themselves as, "Cheeky. We have personality and we're not afraid to show it. We use humour and have a casual way of writing and remain personable." They've also said what they aren't, which is clever, because they've almost created an arch enemy just for their lingo. They're concise, too: "We are fun, but not funny" – there's a big difference between those. "We are cheeky, but not arrogant."

It's a cool way to make the most of your brand and is particularly important if you have a team of staff or outsource quite a lot. In large teams, it's important that everyone is consistent, so that everything you include in your guide is clear to all team members and all outsourced staff, and they are able to get your brand across in a way that is consistent and correlates to your values.

Branded Words – What do We Mean?

PHOTO: INSTAGRAM @THEBODYCOACH

Joe Wicks goes by the title of The Body Coach, and is known for his "Lean in 15" content. He creates 15-minute exercise routines and recipes you can cook in... you guessed it... 15 minutes! Part of his brand is a funny, cheeky, quirkiness. He's a great example of using lingo effectively.

When he creates his meal plans, records videos, or produces content, he has key phrases that only he uses such as: "Guilty!", "In with the Lucy B!" or "In with the midget trees (broccoli)", "Naughty!", "That right there... is lean in 15!" or "Prep like a boss!"

In the short term, Joe uses these words and phrases to get across his cheeky Essex personality. In the long term though, people start to become accustomed to the phrases and can not only identify Joe Wicks just from his words, but they also start to spread the word for him by saying these words themselves. The more he says these phrases, the more WE actually start to use them ourselves, haha!

Wouldn't that be cool if you had your own terms for things and OTHER people started to use them?!

How do you think the term 'Content Marketing' came about? Joe Pulizzi first coined the phrase and now look at how well known it is!

Try it yourself now: Write down a list of terms that you use in your own business to talk about your industry, and come up with your own stylistic lingo, ideally in line with your own brand values and something catchy.

TERM	C O U L D	LINGO
e.g. Broccoli	B E	*e.g. Midget Trees*
	C A	
	L L	
	E D	

KEY TAKEAWAYS FROM MODULE 2: CONTENT BRANDING

We can't stress enough the importance of building a strong brand based on these five key foundational elements:

1. Brand Values
2. Mission Statement
3. Avatar
4. Arch Enemy
5. Lingo

All of these will help you create a firm basis for your brand, and once you start applying these to everything you do and every decision you make, your brand is strengthened. Ask yourself: "Is it in line with my brand values and my mission? Would my arch enemy do this? Can I incorporate my lingo into this?"

We have seen time and time again the incredible impact working all this out has on businesses, business owners, and their bank balance! So if you're reading this book and thinking, "I have a rough idea of what they mean, but I don't have time right now to work on my brand, and it probably won't make much difference," - please dismiss those negative, bad thoughts! It *does* make a difference, so start to work through your brand now before you end up being vanilla, inconsistent and forgettable.

In the next module, we'll be looking at how you can apply your brand to your content, make your mark and put your stamp on the world.

MODULE 3:

CONTENT STAMP

There are over 2,000,000+ blogs written every day, not to mention the videos, podcasts and the trillions of social media posts published too.

How are you going to get noticed and grow your audience amongst all this noise? How are you supposed to compete against your competitors from all around the world, who have bigger resources than you and may have years of content creation already ahead of you?

Since the dawn of time, marketers and business advisors have always spouted that you need to have a USP (Unique Selling Proposition) for your business - something about your business offering that is unique.

Well, we think you ALSO need a 'USP' for your content too! Something that makes your content unique and thus stands it out amongst everyone else's... we call this your Content Stamp. It's about putting your own branded mark onto your content so that it becomes instantly recognisable, brand-building, and highly shareable. It's what's going to make people notice you, come back to you and most importantly tell others about you.

We think this is the most important part of the book, as it's at this point that you will start to tie together the first two modules and can really start to get creative. The fastest-growing companies are the ones who have figured out their unique content stamp, because done correctly, it should resonate with your audience and be highly shareable.

Creating content that is shareable is one of the quickest and cheapest ways to distribute your content and grow your audience. And by shareable, we don't just mean viral cat videos!

To give you a flavour of some brilliant and well-known content stamps and their power, let's take a look at a few examples.

Joe Wicks: He started off making 15 second Instagram videos with recipe ideas done in a cheeky, fast-paced style. No-one else was doing these short, engaging, recipe videos - they had so much personality and were extremely shareable. The idea of 15-minute meals/

exercise resonated with the target audience, and he blew up - now he makes millions and is a TV personality.

John Lee Dumas: John started a daily podcast interviewing the world's most successful entrepreneurs and within 18 months became a multimillionaire. No-one else was really doing a daily podcast in the marketing industry, which was unique, and getting the interviewees to share them afterwards meant that his downloads went through the roof! p.s. Episode 1294 was the best: www.eofire.com/podcast/andrewandpete ;)

DJ Khaled: DJ Khaled was fairly unknown until he started sharing his journey and 'Rules for Success' on Snapchat, just on the cusp of when Snapchat blew up. Now he's creating tracks with the likes of Rhianna and Beyoncé! Lucky guy!

Maybe these examples seem a bit far out and almost too unbelievable, but it's nothing you couldn't have done too! You've had the same tools available to you, so no excuses.

On our membership site, ATOMIC (you should totally check it out), we help people to create their own unique content stamp, so out of the tons of examples let's take a look at a few businesses who've just started this process and see how they're getting on, shall we? You'll see just how well this works for people in the short term as well as the long term - just in case your biggest dream isn't to duet with Beyoncé.

Louise: After just two weeks of going through the Content Mavericks programme on ATOMIC, and defining her brand, Louise immediately started to attract her perfect target audience (fiction authors). Check out how leads from her ideal clients, shot up instantly and quadrupled in 5 months.

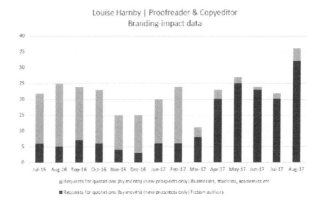

John: John set up his new cleaning company that gives 10% of its profits to supporting charities who are fundraising. Instead of giving tips on how to clean, like you might expect, he actually shares content around how to raise money for charity - incredible! He's won so many contracts already in his first year of business that he's had to start hiring people and has even just franchised his business within 12 months too! Smashing it!

Dave: Dave is highly-sought-after stress and resilience speaker and trainer. His unique content stamp revolves around using cabbages and sprouts as a metaphor to explain stress - bonkers, right?! Not so bonkers when you see how much success he's having. He only works three days a week, and recently he's just been picked up by a talent agent to be an expert on a new TV show!

Do you get the point? Unique content = attention = high growth!

So... are you ready to discover *your* content stamp?!

Yippeeeeee!

THE CONTENT STAMP DISCOVERY TABLE

Coming up with a great idea for your content stamp isn't a five-minute process. It's going to take some time, some brain power and some testing. Having said that, we're going to make it as easy as possible for you.

This is the Content Stamp Discovery Table:

CONTENT STAMP DISCOVERY TABLE				
BRAND	+ ASPIRATIONAL MESSAGE	+ DELIVERY	+ SHAREABILITY	= CONTENT STAMP

We're going to fill out the four empty columns to give you a framework for thinking creatively.

If you think that you're not a creative person, don't worry, because each column, once filled in, will provide you with brainstorming pivots to get your creative juices flowing.

Alternatively, if you are the wildly creative type, this discovery table should provide you with the guidelines to keep you on track, and within some kind of boundaries. We know what you're like!

We want you to read through this, then grab a big piece of paper, a whiteboard or a spreadsheet and come back and work through it properly, filling in each column for yourself.

Let's go through each column so you can see how each one builds up towards your final ideas for potential content stamps. In the first column we have...

BRAND

If you've completed everything from Module 2, you'll have already done a lot of work on your brand, so this step is easy. You'll have your brand values, mission statement, avatar, arch enemy and lingo. Take the essential details from those exercises and plug them into the 'Brand' column.

If you haven't completed all of the branding exercises, take the opportunity now to do these, because we'll be building on them from here. The content stamp step won't work without them.

To make this clearer for you to understand... we'll take two examples, one from a content poor industry and one from a content rich industry, and reverse engineer them - so you get to see the process in action.

Remember, 'content poor' are industries where the potential customer doesn't need to know about how you do what you do, they just want it done for them, e.g. dry cleaners, storage companies, food manufacturers, most products... To succeed, they have to find alternative things to talk about that will actually draw in their potential customers.

Our example for this industry is Chubbies - who predominantly sell shorts, and kick-ass shorts at that! Now shorts aren't all that exciting if you think about it, and there's definitely not much content you can produce around shorts...

Here's how to put shorts on...

Here's how to take shorts off...

Nope, that's not going to do it!

So instead they have created a content stamp all centred around their company mission and 'Aspirational Message', which is all about living life to the max.

Thus, their content is all about escaping the nine to five grind and living life to the fullest, showing you all the cool things you can do at the weekend (...in your shorts of course).

Their blog is called *Chubbies Entertainment* (formerly 'Friday at 5') and they create content about having the best weekend.

Recent posts include:

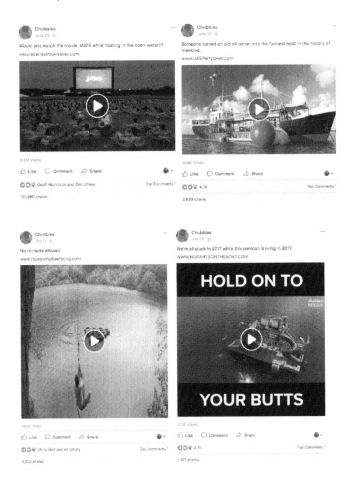

They call their audience 'Chubsters' and they believe that trousers are nothing more than "Leg Prisons" and that everyone needs some "thigh liberation".

What amazing use of lingo there! Hahaha.

This cheeky and quirky brand has exploded their content, their audience and you bet their sales!!

The second example is within a content rich industry. Remember this includes industries like marketing, fitness, HR, who find it much easier to come up with content as they can talk about themselves - but then again so can everyone, so the content landscape is very saturated and noisy.

For this example, we have Joe Wicks, The Body Coach, a cheeky Essex boy who promotes health and fitness. We mentioned Joe Wicks in the last module, but now we'll start to break down why his 'cheeky chappie' content actually works for him.

This is what the Content Stamp Discovery Table looks like once you've filled in the 'Brand' column.

CONTENT STAMP DISCOVERY TABLE: CHUBBIES

BRAND	+ ASPIRATIONAL MESSAGE	+ DELIVERY	+ SHAREABILITY	= CONTENT STAMP
Values: Fun, For The Weekend, Old School **Mission:** Free people from leg prisons (e.g. pants) to have more fun at the weekend **Avatar:** Men around 30, boring office job, 9-5, looking for some fun. **Arch Enemy:** High end fashion company that's super pretentious. Pants. **Lingo:** Voice Characteristics: Informal, Tongue-in-cheek, Retro-cool Brand Words: Leg Prisons, Chubsters, Sky's Out Thighs Out, Thigh Liberation				

CONTENT STAMP DISCOVERY TABLE: THE BODY COACH

BRAND	+ ASPIRATIONAL MESSAGE	+ DELIVERY	+ SHAREABILITY	= CONTENT STAMP
Values: Cheeky, Essex Lad, Aspirational **Mission:** I'm a man on a mission to rescue people from the awful dieting industry. I am sick and tired of people struggling on low calorie diets and meal replacement shakes. **Avatar:** Men & women, under 30, tried diets and shakes, want to eat well, busy people. **Arch Enemy:** Weight Watchers, shake companies **Lingo:** Voice Characteristics: Funny, Conversational, Friendly Brand words: Guilty, Naughty, Lucy B etc.				

(Please note that you only have to fill in the necessities here).

It's important we start with the brand, because your content does need to be consistently portraying your desired image and also needs to be relatable to your target market. However, that will only get you so far. Let's move on to the next column.

ASPIRATIONAL MESSAGE

What is it that your product or service allows people to do AFTER consuming it?

For us, the aspiration after working with us is business growth. We can help you get focussed, come up with a strategy, create great content, grow your list etc, but the ULTIMATE goal is business growth. This is the desire our audience has, so we need to play on that and talk about it in our content.

Defining your Aspirational Message is super important if you are in a content poor industry, because it gives you something to talk about other than your products. This is often a HUGE 'aha' moment for people, because now they have unlocked so much more content!

Referring back to our examples then: the shorts that Chubbies make ALLOW people to go swimming, to be out in hot weather, to give the impression that they are a fun, outgoing person.

Chubbies' aspirational message is therefore to help people get outside more and have fun. So that's exactly what their content is all about; they don't talk about what their shorts are made of, how to choose shorts, or how to wear them, because people don't care about that! What they do care about is what your product or service ALLOWS them to do. It's playing on the Avatar's problems, emotions and social desires.

Looking at the Chubbies Entertainment blog, we can see that they get to the heart of their avatar's desires very well. Their avatar is likely to be a guy stuck in an office Monday to Friday, and when he gets to the weekend he wants to let loose, and more importantly LOOK like the fun guy on all those Facebook posts. Chubbies shorts allow him to do that, but so does their content, because it gives a ton of fun ideas he can do at the weekend (while wearing shorts).

They have a 'Manifesto' page, where shoppers can find out exactly what the brand stands for. They say: "Chubbies is to the weekend what peanut butter is to jelly. They exist to bring you the best weekend clothes that have ever been conceived. They hate pants and long shorts, because they hide your legs."

It's all about freedom and relaxation (not just shorts!) and the absence of pretence. They could have blogged about fashion trends instead, but they thought that the fashion industry was a bit stuck up, so they wanted to disrupt it and have some fun with it. You can visit their website to get a better idea of what they do and how they do it.

Their aspirational message, again from their website, says: "It's so awesome that so many people out there are potentially having ever so slightly better, fuller weekends and creating more weekend memories because of something we're doing. It's all about fun, freedom and doing whatever the hell you want with the people you love. And the Chubster nation is proof that the weekend is alive and well."

They're operating in a content poor industry, but have created so much content around their aspirational message, and it's paying off big time for them. So, think about what your aspirational message is and think about how that could result in you talking about a whole lot more than just your products/services.

On the flip side, you can see how it also helps content rich industries too.

Joe Wicks' aspirational message comes from the mission statement on his site. "It's about not starving yourself, having fun with cooking rather than viewing it as a chore, and avoiding microwave meals. It's about getting sexy and lean, and making it easy, quick and sustainable for busy people." i.e. I want to be a young, successful, lean person, full of energy, just like Joe.

After you buy Joe's services, you want to feel sexier and more confident. To do that though, you need to be able to fit regular exercise and eating healthily into your busy schedule.

From this Joe COULD have started to talk more about ways to feel more confident, how to chat up women, how to get more done in the day... but instead he focussed on talking about what he's good at (exercise and healthy eating) but doing it in a way that would resonate with his audience.

This is what Joe's content is all based upon: quick (15 minute) meals and exercise routines that busy people can do to make themselves look lean and sexy. Joe can still talk about his industry, unlike content poor companies, but this aspirational message defines HOW he does that. So instead of creating a standard blog on recipes that typically take 45 minutes, he produces content in fast-paced, 15-second videos about 15-minute meals. Boom!

So if you're content poor, your aspirational message impacts on WHAT you talk about that sets you apart from your 'boring' industry.

And with content rich industries, your aspirational message impacts more on HOW you say it to set you apart from the rest of your heavily saturated industry.

Work on your aspirational message now. What does your offering allow people to do, and how can you help people with that through your content too?

Stick your aspirational message into the table like so:

CONTENT STAMP DISCOVERY TABLE: CHUBBIES

BRAND	+ ASPIRATIONAL MESSAGE	+ DELIVERY	+ SHAREABILITY	= CONTENT STAMP
Values: Fun, For The Weekend, Old School **Mission:** Free people from leg prisons (e.g. pants) to have more fun at the weekend **Avatar:** Men around 30, boring office job, 9-5, looking for some fun. **Arch Enemy:** High end fashion company that's super pretentious. Pants. **Lingo:** Voice Characteristics: Informal, Tongue-in-cheek, Retro-cool Brand Words: Leg Prisons, Chubsters, Sky's Out Thighs Out, Thigh Liberation	**Live for the weekend** **Take off your pants, throw on some shorts and have fun** **Get your legs out at the weekend for a great time** **The 'Friday at 5' feeling** **From their website:** "It's so awesome that so many people out there are potentially having ever-so-slightly better, more full weekends -- and creating more weekend memories because of something we're doing. It's all about fun, freedom, and doing whatever the hell you want with the people you love, and the Chubster Nation is proof that the weekend is alive and well."			

CONTENT STAMP DISCOVERY TABLE: THE BODY COACH

BRAND	+ ASPIRATIONAL MESSAGE	+ DELIVERY	+ SHAREABILITY	= CONTENT STAMP
Values: Cheeky, Essex Lad, Aspirational **Mission:** I'm a man on a mission to rescue people from the awful dieting industry. I am sick and tired of people struggling on low calorie diets and meal replacement shakes. **Avatar:** Men & women, under 30, tried diets and shakes, want to eat well, busy people. **Arch Enemy:** Weight Watchers, shake companies **Lingo:** Voice Characteristics: Funny, Conversational, Friendly Brand words: Guilty, Naughty, Lucy B etc.	**Stop starving yourself** **Have fun cooking** **Get lean** **Get sexy** **Stay that way** **Stop struggling** **Easy, quick and sustainable** **Even busy people can do this**			

Next up we have...

DELIVERY

How are you going to deliver your primary rich content? Think about the medium and the platform. There are only a limited number of channels on which you can create and distribute your content, but you need to be KNOWN for just one of them as this makes it easy to tell others about you. i.e. 'Have you checked out EOFire, it's a daily podcast', 'check out Joe Wicks on Instagram - he does these fun little recipe videos'...

Here are some options to think about:

WRITTEN WORD
Blog, Tumblr, LinkedIn Publisher, Medium etc.

VIDEO
YouTube, Instagram, Facebook, Vimeo, Snapchat

LIVE VIDEO
Facebook Live, Periscope, webinars

VISUAL
Infographics, SlideShare, Instagram, Pinterest

AUDIO

Podcasts, audio blogs, SoundCloud, Anchor

So which should you choose?

Where most people go wrong here is that they choose the medium *they* are most comfortable with, rather than considering how their avatar would prefer to consume their content.

Yes, to a degree it's good to do something that you're more comfortable with, BUT you're constantly going to be swimming upstream. People told us all the time that we'd be great on video and that video is where we should be, but we held back for years because we weren't comfortable on camera and we didn't have the confidence or the knowledge about how to do it. The moment we bit the bullet and did it anyway, life got waaayyy easier!

Instantly we got more sales, subscribers, speaking gigs, and fan mail - from real fans! Fans who were people we'd never met before from all over the world! It was incredible, and we've always kicked ourselves for not doing it sooner.

So where would you thrive creating content, and more importantly how does your avatar take their content?

Do they listen to podcasts while driving to work? Do they read blogs on their phones at lunch time? Do they watch webinars whilst making dinner? Do they binge watch YouTube videos before bed?

If you're finding it hard to think of the answers, you might need to go back to your avatar and do some more research.

Instagram is stereotypically quite an image-conscious platform for the younger 'trendy' millennial, but also one which has had bad press for unrealistic portrayal of body shapes. This is a great place for the Joe Wicks brand, because it's all about getting fit and lean naturally, feeling good and having fun. So when Instagram released the ability to do 15-second videos on its platform, Joe was all over it. It was the perfect place for his avatar to hang out, and he could get across his brand through video.

For Chubbies it's all about their Facebook Page. Facebook is the type of place to post up photos of your weekend whilst attempting to make everyone jealous - right?! This is perfect for Chubbies, because this is where their audience hangs out and shares all the fun stuff they're doing or want to do.

Chubbies will send out emails to their blog, but the main call to action (what action they want the readers to take) on the blog is always to share it on Facebook - where they get most of their interaction. On Facebook they have over 1.6 million fans, and they regularly post amazing native videos there, which gets them the most interaction over their blog and YouTube channel.

Just to explain: Native video is when you post or upload a video to the platform rather than pasting a link on, for instance, your Facebook page, which directs people elsewhere and away from Facebook e.g. to a blog or a YouTube video.

Chubbies are using Facebook because that's where their audience hangs out and they use video because it's the best way to show off having fun. Facebook also LOVES native video!!

As we've said, Instagram worked for Joe Wicks because many of the users are image-conscious and on-trend. He used the 15 second video limit to his advantage to stand out.

Think about the limitations in the platform you're using and how you can use that to your advantage. There are some amazing storytellers on Snapchat, for example, and it's the most awkward platform there is. You've only got 10 seconds and your content also disappears, but the limitation inspires creativity.

So where does your avatar hang out and how do they want to take their content?

Add in your content delivery method now to the Content Stamp Discovery Table.

BRAND	+ ASPIRATIONAL MESSAGE	+ DELIVERY	+ SHAREABILITY	= CONTENT STAMP
Values: Fun, For The Weekend, Old School **Mission:** Free people from leg prisons (e.g. pants) to have more fun at the weekend **Avatar:** Men around 30, boring office job, 9-5, looking for some fun. **Arch Enemy:** High end fashion company that's super pretentious. Pants. **Lingo:** Voice Characteristics: Informal, Tongue-in-cheek, Retro-cool Brand Words: Leg Prisons, Chubsters, Sky's Out Thighs Out, Thigh Liberation	**Live for the weekend** **Take off your pants, throw on some shorts and have fun** **Get your legs out at the weekend for a great time** **The 'Friday at 5' feeling** **From their website:** "It's so awesome that so many people out there are potentially having ever-so-slightly better, more full weekends -- and creating more weekend memories because of something we're doing. It's all about fun, freedom, and doing whatever the hell you want with the people you love, and the Chubster Nation is proof that the weekend is alive and well."	Facebook Page - native video content. That's where their audience likes to share what they're doing at the weekend, and their fun plans. Blog - for linking - to get people back to their website		

CONTENT STAMP DISCOVERY TABLE: THE BODY COACH

BRAND	+ ASPIRATIONAL MESSAGE	+ DELIVERY	+ SHAREABILITY	= CONTENT STAMP
Values: Cheeky, Essex Lad, Aspirational **Mission:** I'm a man on a mission to rescue people from the awful dieting industry. I am sick and tired of people struggling on low calorie diets and meal replacement shakes. **Avatar:** Men & women, under 30, tried diets and shakes, want to eat well, busy people. **Arch Enemy:** Weight Watchers, shake companies **Lingo:** Voice Characteristics: Funny, Conversational, Friendly Brand words: Guilty, Naughty, Lucy B etc.	**Stop starving yourself** **Have fun cooking** **Get lean** **Get sexy** **Stay that way** **Stop struggling** **Easy, quick and sustainable** **Even busy people can do this**	Instagram - a couple years ago - where trendy young, image conscious were. 15 Second limit - used this limitation to stand out. Now - Facebook & Snapchat (where the audience is).		

SHAREABILITY

Why are people going to share your content?

Creating highly shareable content is the quickest way to grow your audience, subscribers and consequently your **sales**.

When your content gets shared, you get in front of a whole new audience, and you gain masses of social proof too.

Social media has been dubbed 'pay to play', but the more highly engaging and shareable content you have, the less you need to rely on paying for reach (how many people see your posts) as your content will do the job for you.

But it's easier said than done, right?!

Content's a BEACH!

Say that aloud and you get the idea... creating highly shareable and engaging content is tough!

You put all this effort into crafting the perfect posts, researching, writing, proofreading, publishing and promoting... and what happens? Content Crickets! Well, no more!

There are five fundamental reasons why people are going to share your content on social and it comes in an easy to remember acronym, which funnily enough is: BEACH

That's right, BEACH actually stands for something! That's why content really is a BEACH! :D

So here you go, the five reasons why people will share, so that you can start to blow up your content!

B is for Brand Advocacy

People will simply share your content because they are fans of your brand.

Let us tell you a story about this, and not just any kind of story... a loooove story.

But not the '50 Shades of ...' kind of love story! Haha.

Once upon a time, we were doing a live broadcast on Periscope after Social Media Marketing World 2016, and there was a lady watching live who was really enjoying all of our tips.

We won't tell you her name, but in the spirit of 50 Shades, let's call her Lady Grey!

After the broadcast, Lady Grey sent us a message saying how much she enjoyed our Periscope.

The typical thing to do here is reply, "Thanks Lady Grey! Really appreciate that, have a great day!"

BUT INSTEAD we recorded a Twitter video reply to her saying thank you, and asking her questions about her business too, which led to a great conversation.

You know what, she LOVED IT! She loved the fact that we'd taken the time to record a personalised video just to her, and that we took an interest in her. What followed then shocked us.

We started to see over the next few days, weeks and months that she would Like, Comment, and Retweet EVERYTHING we Tweeted. In fact, she'd even go on our blog and share our blogs too.

She fell in love with our brand. She was now a brand advocate.

But we wanted more.

We are marketers after all!

What if we could replicate this? What if today we had just one person Retweeting everything we did, then tomorrow we had two people, and three the next day... what if after six months we had hundreds of people Retweeting us, how cool would that be?!

Wouldn't you like that too?

Top Tips to Creating More Brand Advocates

Be Proactive

You might not be a big influencer with loads of people saying how great you are yet, so what you need to do is get out there, find your perfect clients and engage with them FIRST!

Too many people are lazy when it comes to social and only reply to comments, rather than go out there and comment on other people's posts first.

If you want to create new relationships and keep up with existing ones, make regular time in your diary to proactively go out and interact with people.

There's a great tool called 'Cloze' which assesses your social following and emails and tells you who you need to keep in touch with on a regular basis.

Remember that the algorithms on social media platforms now give preference to posts from people who you interact more with... **thus the more conversations you're having, the more reach you're going to get on your posts.** Simply because, if people are interacting with your content/account, the algorithms will show more of your posts to them. It makes sense, so let's use this to our advantage!

Be Reliable

Brand advocates will share your content even without reading it in most cases - because they know what to expect from your content. They know the style, they know it will be great quality and they blindly trust you enough to share it without even reading.

This ONLY comes from being there for them consistently over time. So keep up the good work, try your best with every post, don't get lazy, and show up regularly. Be someone they can rely on every time to create content they love.

Have a Mission

No one can be a fan of someone who's just out to make money. What do you stand for that your audience can get behind? This ties back into your Mission from Module 2 :)

Let Them In

People can't be fans of people they don't really know, so let them in a little bit more. Tell your story, share things with your audience that you might only tell your friends, be humble and modest rather than bragging, tell people your flaws and allow them to feel something for you.

Also show them your face more! People can get behind a face more than a logo, we learnt this in a big way when we started our YouTube channel (www.youtube.com/andrewandpeteTV). Our fans shot up the more we put our faces out there.

Brand Advocacy: If you want more shares, create more fans.

E is for Emotion

If we can tap into emotions we unlock the power to move people into action.

Pete's brother, John, was doing an epic run for charity - seven marathons in seven days. It's an incredibly tough feat, most people couldn't bear to run one marathon, never mind seven in a row! It was a huge challenge but one he was doing for a good cause.

John calls Pete one day in distress and says, "Bro, you do marketing or something right?"

(Haha thanks brother!)

"Yeh, how can I help" I said.

John, "I'm killing myself here, I'm working 80-hour weeks with my job that's stressing me out, I'm trying to fit in time to train for these marathons, I've got to eat, sleep and on top of that raise some money. Thing is, I've been trying to raise some money for like six months and I'm getting nowhere! What do I do?! I'm running out of time!"

He'd built up his Facebook page to over 200 likes, but do you know how much money he'd raised in six months?

£10. (that's $12.90 for you Americans)

OUCH!!

It just wasn't worth it.

He'd poured his heart out to me, so I told him to do just that on video. Tell your story, show your audience how much effort you're really putting into it, what it means to you, show the training high altitude simulation mask you have to wear, show the miserable weather you're out in... be honest, raw and open.

So that's what he did.

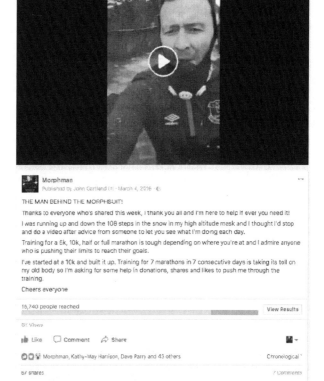

Morphman
Published by John Gartland [?] · March 4, 2016 · 🌐

THE MAN BEHIND THE MORPHSUIT!

Thanks to everyone who's shared this week, I thank you all and I'm here to help if ever you need it!

I was running up and down the 108 steps in the snow in my high altitude mask and I thought I'd stop and do a video after advice from someone to let you see what I'm doing each day.

Training for a 5k, 10k, half or full marathon is tough depending on where you're at and I admire anyone who is pushing their limits to reach their goals.

I've started at a 10k and built it up. Training for 7 marathons in 7 consecutive days is taking its toll on my old body so I'm asking for some help in donations, shares and likes to push me through the training.

Cheers everyone

16,740 people reached   View Results

6K Views

👍 Like   💬 Comment   ↗ Share   🖼 ▾

👍😮❤ Morphman, Kathy-May Harrison, Dave Parry and 43 others   Chronological ˅

67 shares   7 Comments

Overnight the video on his tiny page got over 60 shares, 6,000 views, and reached over 10,000 people! It then got picked up by a page with over a million page likes and got a ton more engagement there.

Overnight he received just under $4,000 in donations. Wow!

He then got picked up by the beer brand Coors Light, who went on to sponsor John for even more money!

Incredible. It just goes to show what a little emotion can do for you.

But there are lots of different emotions you can tap into:

WHAT EMOTIONS CAN WE TAP INTO?

LOVE	DISGUST	SURPRISE
JOY	ANGER	SHOCK
CURIOSITY	AWE	ENVY
NOSTALGIA	FEAR	SERENITY
HUMOUR	ANTICIPATION	AMAZEMENT

You've got no excuse for creating vanilla content when you can tap into all these different emotions.

But which is the best emotion that will drive the highest number of shares?

It's the more 'High Arousal' emotions that always perform the best. And NO, we don't mean *like that!* We're falling into 50 shades of social media again here haha.

What we mean by that is, the more extreme the emotion, the more it *moves* people.

e.g. Something that makes you mildly amused isn't going to make you share as much as something that has you rolling around laughing.

Something that makes you mildly discontent has less power than something that makes you really disgusted and frustrated. You see the difference?

Emotion: If you want more shares, tap into high arousal emotions.

A is for Appearance

Everybody wants to look good in front of their peers, it's just natural.

People will only share content online that aids them in their goal of portraying themselves in the way they want to be seen, whether that's helpful, caring, funny, in the know, smart, sexy, trendy and so on.

So, we need to reverse engineer this and think about how we can create content that makes our audience look good by sharing it.

Social Media Examiner knows that its target market (budding social media experts) want to look more 'in the know' and knowledgeable to their audience, so what do they do? They create highly-in-depth how-to articles and post about the latest features/breaking news on social media, thus making their audience look like they're keeping up with current trends and features by sharing.

Appearance: If you want more shares, help your audience look good by sharing your content.

C is for Causes & Beliefs

If you can align your brand to something your audience is passionate about and cares about then you hold the power to be shared. This is Cause-Based Content Marketing.

Uber did a great campaign with this idea. They teamed up with Mothers Against Drunk Driving (MADD) - a charity supporting those who have lost loved ones due to drunk drivers and raising awareness to reduce drink driving. They beautifully executed the cause-based content marketing approach with a July 4th Independence Day campaign. For the July 4th weekend, Uber promoted a unique discount code that, when redeemed, resulted in a $1 donation to MADD ($10 for new customers).

They produced a series of blogs about it, they held a press conference and they had a hashtag: #LeaveTheKeys - and did this get shared? Yes! Just think of all the people whose lives had been impacted by drink drivers and everyone who just wants to promote safe driving. Of course they're going to share the message because it's so important to them, and every time they do, they're also spreading the good word about Uber.

How Can You Apply This to Your Business?

Success in this arena is all about developing the right strategy and executing it in an authentic, organic way that brings mutual benefit to everyone involved. So it needs to be **real** - there's no point in just picking a random charity that you don't care about, because that lack of authenticity will come across. BUT it also needs to support something **relevant** to your business and audience.

With Uber - their product IS the solution to the cause, the hashtag #LeaveTheKeys is really just #BookAnUber in disguise!

So what are the issues and causes that are important to you AND your audience? Remember, it doesn't just have to be charity based, it can be any mission that you feel strongly about.

Causes and Beliefs: If you want more shares, align your brand to a cause that is both real and relevant

H is for High Value

You've probably heard of this one before... 'givers gain'. We're all trying to produce quality, valuable content yes?

But we're here to push you on that.

When we first got the opportunity to write for Social Media Examiner - a world-leading publication in our industry, what do you think we did?

We went all out! We did a ton of research, we created unique GIFs for it, we made images, we edited it and proofread it over and over again and it was super in-depth. It was one of the best articles we'd ever written. We spent weeks on it.

And did it get shared?

Yeh! A ton! It went down so well, and we were extremely chuffed.

BUT, hang on a minute...

Why are we putting that much effort into this guest blog and not OUR OWN content?!

We were only spending 30 minutes to two hours on our own content. No wonder our own blog wasn't taking off!

It was from this moment on that we decided to put more effort into making our content better and giving as much value as we could.

Straight away we saw enormous benefits of doing this: more shares than ever, more fans, more subscribers and more customers!

That realisation was a big shock to our system. So our question to you is, really think about how much value you are giving with your content. How can you add even more value?

Go the extra mile, it's never crowded.

High Value: If you want more shares, the more valuable your content needs to be.

Content's a BEACH

To summarise then:

Brand Advocacy: *If you want more shares, create more fans*
Emotion: *If you want more shares, tap into high arousal emotions*
Appearance: *If you want more shares, help your audience to look good by sharing your content*
Causes and Beliefs: *If you want more shares, align your brand to a cause that is both real and relevant*
High Value: *The more shares you want, the more valuable your content needs to be*

Whack these titles into your Discovery Table and start coming up with ideas of how you can make your content more shareable. You don't have to hit ALL of the points, but the more you do, the better.

Human Shareability vs. Algorithm Shareability

The ideas above have been all human focussed - why do *people* share.

But, if we want maximum shareability we ALSO need to play into the algorithm's hands too.
At any one time, social networks could show you thousands of posts, so they need algorithms to serve

you the content that they consider to be the most relevant and engaging to you. It makes sense, because that's all they want - for you to log in and stay on there as long as possible. The longer you are on their platform, the more money they make from the data they get from you and the ads they can serve you whilst browsing.

Therefore, **social media algorithms** that decide what content and posts get seen and which don't also now play a **huge factor in how shareable your content can be.**

For example, if you post on Facebook with a link, you will get less reach than if you didn't. If your post gets a lot of engagement, Facebook will distribute that post further and give you higher reach.

So the word 'shareable' now doesn't only incorporate when someone physically shares your posts but also includes by how much the algorithms share your posts in people's timelines too :O

With this in mind, what factors affect the social media algorithms? More importantly, how can we use them to our advantage when posting to get more organic reach and to get more of our content shared?

To keep this fresh, we've made a pdf for you which you can download for free which talks about these algorithms and gives you a ton of hacks to get more reach. After implementing these ideas our reach on Facebook alone has gone up from around 2-50 people reached (so incredibly dismal!) to consistently between 400-5,000 people reached. Heck, it pays off to play into the algorithms hands!

The pdf covers all the main platforms and also includes posts that you can steal and use for yourself. Download it for free here: www.andrewandpete.com/33hacks

THE CONTENT STAMP DISCOVERY PROCESS

Once you've got the first four columns of the table filled in, you've built your framework for coming up with ideas to create your on-brand, aspirational and shareable content stamp. The information you've filled in each column now becomes a 'Brainstorming Pivot' - something to spark or trigger new ideas and trains of thought. Creativity becomes easier once you have something to trigger those ideas.

It's time to use this framework to brainstorm awesome ideas for your potential content stamp! We're going to write down all the potential ideas in that final column and from there, choose only one to go ahead with!

Remember a content stamp is that ONE thing that you're known for, something that others can easily spread. A sign of a good content stamp is being able to tell others about it in five seconds or less:

Andrew and Pete: Fun but helpful vlog
EOFire: Daily podcast interviewing the world's most successful and inspiring entrepreneurs
Chubbies: Fun videos on Facebook about what to do at the weekend
Joe Wicks: 15 second Instagram recipes

Let's look at our two examples and how they could have used the discovery table.

CONTENT STAMP DISCOVERY TABLE: THE BODY COACH

BRAND	+ ASPIRATIONAL MESSAGE	+ DELIVERY	+ SHAREABILITY	= CONTENT STAMP
Values: Cheeky, Essex Lad, Aspirational **Mission:** I'm a man on a mission to rescue people from the awful dieting industry. I am sick and tired of people struggling on low calorie diets and meal replacement shakes. **Avatar:** Men & women, under 30, tried diets and shakes, want to eat well, busy people. **Arch Enemy:** Weight Watchers, shake companies **Lingo:** Voice Characteristics: Funny, Conversational, Friendly Brand words: Guilty, Naughty, Lucy B etc.	**Stop starving yourself** Have fun cooking **Get lean** **Get sexy** **Stay that way** **Stop struggling** **Easy, quick and sustainable** **Even busy people can do this**	Instagram - a couple years ago - where trendy young, image conscious were. 15 Second limit - used this limitation to stand out. Now - Facebook & Snapchat (where the audience is).	**BRAND ADVOCACY** Joe isnt your standard posh chef. He's an Essex lad, and acts like your mates **EMOTION** You're laughing but you're also impressed with the ideas **APPEARANCE** You look like the healthy one when sharing your Lean in 15 creations **CAUSES AND BELIEFS** Being healthier is better. Getting more people active. **HIGH VALUE** Where else can you get amazing ideas delivered that quick!	15 Second Instagram videos, fun and fast paced, cheeky Essex style.

The brainstorming pivots Joe Wicks would have pulled out would be to do something for busy people, something on Instagram, and something cheeky and humorous... So, short, fun, healthy recipes on Instagram is what he'd write in the content stamp column. See how that works?

Many more ideas could have come about too... Spoof adverts for shake companies? Skits on bad diets? Educational but funny videos on why diets don't work and you're wasting time? Workouts in funny places, for people who are pushed for time and don't have the luxury of the gym? Case studies where two foods go head to head?

Hopefully you're starting to see the potential of this model and the framework for your creativity. It's simply applying each of the elements and mixing and matching them to come up with exciting ideas.

CONTENT STAMP DISCOVERY TABLE: CHUBBIES

BRAND	+ ASPIRATIONAL MESSAGE	+ DELIVERY	+ SHAREABILITY	= CONTENT STAMP
Values: Fun, For The Weekend, Old School	Live for the weekend	Facebook Page - native video content That's where their audience likes to share what they're doing at the weekend, and their fun plans.	**BRAND ADVOCACY**	Fun videos on Facebook based around the aspirational message of living life at the weekend.
Mission: Free people from leg prisons (e.g. pants) to have more fun at the weekend	**Take off your pants, throw on some shorts and have fun**		**EMOTION** Funny content, but also 'awe' - so many amazing things you didn't know you could do	
Avatar: Men around 30, boring office job, 9-5, looking for some fun.	**Get your legs out at the weekend for a great time**	Blog - for linking - to get people back to their website	**APPEARANCE** You look like the fun one when you share this content	
	The 'Friday at 5' feeling			
Arch Enemy: High end fashion company that's super pretentious. Pants.	**From their website:** "It's so awesome that so many people out there are potentially having ever-so-slightly better, more full weekends -- and creating more weekend memories because of something we're doing. It's all about fun, freedom, and doing whatever the hell you want with the people you love, and the Chubster Nation is proof that the weekend is alive and well."		**CAUSES AND BELIEFS** The weekend is for living! Anti 9-5 boring life. Throw on some shorts and have some fun	
Lingo: Voice Characteristics: Informal, Tongue-in-Cheek, Retro-cool			**HIGH VALUE**	
Brand Words: Leg Prisons, Chubsters, Sky's Out Thighs Out, Thigh Liberation				

Chubbies' content stamp is all about 'appearance' - it makes people look good! By sharing videos all about fun stuff you can do at the weekend (in your shorts), it gives people a chance to build their own social currency by sharing it. It's cool, fun content that if you were to share, would also make you look fun in front of your friends. This highly sharable element of their content has served them well!

Your turn!

Now it's your turn. Fill in each of the columns and start to get your creative juices flowing!

To keep you on track, here are a few ideas to help you work through the process.

1. Mix and match your brainstorming pivot points: Take little bits from each of the columns – e.g. busy people, humour, Instagram – and think about what you could do around each one

2. Ask questions: Go off and ask yourself questions surrounding each pivot, such as, "How can I create something humorous for Instagram?"

3. Write ideas down: You have to write ALL of your ideas down, no matter how atrocious they sound. If you don't, it'll be stuck in your head and you won't be able to think about anything else. Get it down and out of your head and move on quickly to the next idea

4. Take one idea at a time: Go through your list of ideas and take one at a time, starting with those that you think have the most potential

5. Include all four aspects: Go through each of the four aspects (brand, aspirational message, shareability and deliverability) and try to get them all into your content planning

6. Get a friend to help: Oftentimes it's best to brainstorm with others who you can bounce ideas off and build on from one another

7. REPEAT! Repeat the process until you have a lot of cool, unique ideas

How do You Choose 'The One'?

If you do this properly you should come up with lots of potential stamp ideas. But which one is going to serve you best? Go with the one you think has the most potential, and give it a good go. Put your all into it and try it a few times. If it doesn't get a good reaction, try another one of your ideas!

The temptation is again to go with what you know and something you're comfortable with. Remember it's not about what's easiest for *you*, it's about what your customer wants.

Don't be afraid to try new stuff either. Some of the best content stamps were based on new platforms, new technology and new features. We are at an exciting point right now where innovation is happening faster than ever and being ahead of the curve is always a good thing!

Analytics vs Reaction

What a lot of people want to do is to just go straight to quantitative data, we get that. Making decisions based on data is the smart thing to do!

However, in the early stages, especially if you don't have a huge audience or following, then data is limiting, and relying on it may make for poor decisions being made.

We don't want you to get bogged down worrying about every metric under the sun. There are three main stages of your content marketing journey, and depending on which stage you're at, you only need to be thinking about a few metrics at a time!

Stage 1: Engagement

When you start you out you want to be looking predominantly at getting some kind of reaction... comments, likes, shares, emails from people, face to face reactions etc.

The reality is, if you're just getting started with content marketing, it's not the impact on sales you need to be looking at, it's engagement!

If you're not getting comments, likes and shares, even when you have a tiny audience, there is no point continuing to put the time, effort, and money into distributing and promoting your content as it is - you will just be hitting your head against the wall. You're just going to bore or annoy people.

So at the beginning you need to focus on trying different things, to make your content stamp unique and remarkable so that it DOES get some kind of reaction - and we don't just mean from friends and family!

It can be quite qualitative in the beginning, which might be frustrating for some of you data nerds, but ignoring qualitative reactions and gut feeling can be dangerous.

It's not that you aren't going to generate sales from content in Stage One - you will if you're doing it right, but we're not getting ourselves bogged down in sales metrics yet!

Stage 2: Audience Growth

Once you have your unique content stamp that people are engaging with, it's now worth actually investing more of your time and money into distribution of your content - because you know it's going to stick!

You should be looking at key metrics that measure your audience growth, including: Views, Subscribers, Loyalty, and Consistency (yours).

The four main factors that limit your growth here are:

1. **Remarkability** - Are people sharing your content? If not go back to your content stamp
2. **Consistency** - Consistently posting increases trust and the likelihood that people will subscribe and keep coming back for regular updates
3. **Frequency** - The more you publish, the more you have to draw people in. Are you still only blogging once a month? Think about ramping it up big time! We'll help you with this in Module 5

4. **Distribution** - Are you utilising all the tools at your disposal? We'll help you with this in Module 6

Stage 3: Monetisation

This is the juicy bit that everyone skips ahead to, but a growing, loyal audience is much easier to monetise than one which is still pretty cold.

The key metrics here depend on your monetisation methods, but let's say for example you have an online course. *The metrics you want to keep a close eye on include things like traffic to landing page, clicks to the checkout and cart abandonment, total number of sales, repeat sales.*

The steps are working out how you are turning your content into sales, and what the key steps are that a potential customer goes through before buying. In Module 7, we'll be mapping this out.

All the tools you'll be using should have analytics built in, but a nice catch-all is Google Analytics, specifically their 'Conversion Goals'. You basically tell Google Analytics which page of your website a web visitor needs to land on to be tracked as a 'conversion' (for example, a *thank you* page after purchasing). Google will then be able to tell you what content on your site is drawing in the most traffic and which bits of content inspire the most actions to purchasing.

It's important to know where you are at on these three stages, because it's very easy to beat yourself up if you're trying to measure against sales straight away.

KEY TAKEAWAYS FROM MODULE 3: CONTENT STAMP

At the end of the day, you're going to struggle if you're producing average, vanilla, same-y content. If you're just doing what everyone else is doing you're ALWAYS going to be one step behind.

"You can't get ahead by following others."

So it might seem like a lot of hard work to fill out this discovery table, but it's going to save you from years of swimming upstream and getting poor results from your content creation.

Put in the effort now and it will pay off going forward. As we always say, "Creativity beats budget".

Creating content should also be enjoyable for you to do! If it's not, you're going to find it difficult to be consistent, as your motivation will fade over time. That warrants another Andrew and Pete quote! Three in a row, haha:

"You will never create content consistently if you don't enjoy it."

If you're unsure of the level of content you need to produce then the next section is going to help you. If you are worried about this taking too long, then don't worry - that's what Module 5: Content Organisation is all about ;). We got your back!

We're now going to add a piece to the Content Mission Statement, so it reads:

I'm going to create content for _____ so that they can _____, because _____. To do this, my Content Stamp will be _____.

MODULE 4:

CONTENT CREATION

Rightio then... at this point you understand why you need to be doing this, you have a killer brand ready to unleash on the world and a Content STAMP to match, now our friend... it is time to start creating!!!

Buckle up!

YOUR DELIVERY

In the last module, we talked about the five different delivery methods:

- Written
- Audio
- Visual
- Video
- Live Video

If you've been actioning this book up until this point, you should be clear by now on how your avatar 'takes their content' and have a solid idea as to your content stamp.

Before you start creating, however, let's get clear on how and what you are going to start creating.

There's More to This Than Blogging

We're not here to bash the blog - there's a ton of industries and avatars where writing a blog may still be the best option. Blogging is amazing for SEO, Google loves them, and there are a ton of reasons why blogging may be great for your business.

Saying that, nowadays it's not always the logical place to start!

The blog kick-started the 'content marketing' movement. With slow internet dial-up, written walls of text were all we had as marketers to communicate online, and the 'blog' quickly became the norm.

Because of this, when we talk to business owners about content marketing, a lot of them have already started blogging, without any thought for the other mediums.

The biggest downside to blogging, in our opinion, is the effort involved from the consumers - they have to actually read it! How many blogs have you bookmarked to 'come back to when you have time' to have never ever gone back to them again?

Be honest now ;)

The other content mediums take less effort to consume, which is why we like them.

You can listen to a podcast doing squats.

Flick through Instagram whilst watching Game of Thrones.

Watch a YouTube video in the bath, or in bed next to your sleeping partner (we have been sent photos of people doing this #inbedwithAnP).

So just to reiterate - deciding on your content medium should be down to your avatar, and if you are a bit stuck at this stage, go back and flesh out your avatar more, even potentially talking to them can help see what they want.

CONTENT STANDARDS

All content wasn't created equal.

We define 'content standards' as the components that make up your piece of content rather than the information itself. Things like audio quality, text size, readability, editing etc.

Your knowledge on your chosen subject may be spot-on, but if it is presented in a 'poor' format then it's not going to catch on.

This is where content standards come into play. You must understand what the expected standard is and how to compete with it. We aren't asking you to chase perfection here, but just have something to judge your content against, and more importantly - aim for.

Follow the Leader of the Medium, not the Field

What most people will do at this stage is look to see who is the leader in their field and in a particular medium. If you are an accountant wanting to launch a podcast, you may be tempted to search for all the other accountants who have a podcast and see what they are doing.

This sounds sensible, right? Let's see what the competition are up to, and make sure our podcast is better than theirs. However, those accountants probably don't have the best podcasts in the world.

What would be an even better idea is to search for the most listened-to podcasts of all time, and see what they do. Their content standards are probably much higher than your competitors, and therefore a much better place to draw some inspiration from.

When we decided to launch our YouTube channel, of course we checked out other marketers to see what they were doing, but we didn't want to be a carbon-copy of them. When it came to making decisions like:

- Editing style
- Thumbnail design
- Signs offs
- Introductions
- Etc

We were following the leaders of the medium, not our field, i.e. popular YouTubers, because they've set the benchmark of quality in this medium and proven what it takes.

Side note: You're going to want to keep your avatar in mind here too. We're drawing inspiration from the leaders of the medium for our content standards, but we're not copying their content - as that is most likely aimed at a completely different audience. Understanding that distinction is important, otherwise you'll all go away and create insane prank videos.

WRITTEN WORDS: CONTENT STANDARDS

If you thought that nothing much could go wrong with blogging, you would be wrong.

Your information may be the best out there, but there are so many ways your blogs can fall down when it comes to production, that will turn readers off.

Here are some things to be wary of...

Font Size: 17 is the new 12. Use a slightly bigger font size than what you are used to. This will reduce the amount of words per line and make the blog look more readable.

75% Width: Don't have your blog run the entire length of your website, again it will look much harder to read. Your blog should be maximum 75% across the width of your site. Having a sidebar is a common way to accomplish this. Also, having a sidebar gives you extra space for lead magnets, ads, and other content you want readers to click on.

Increased Line Spacing: Many website themes allow you to play with the line spacing. Increasing it slightly will increase the aesthetics of your posts.

These three things will most likely be controlled in your website settings, or if you are using WordPress some themes will allow you to alter these.

Avoid Walls of Text: Break up your articles into short paragraphs, use subtitles and include other multi-media where possible within the blog. You should include images, GIFs, videos, embedded Tweets, embedded audio bites, Tweetables and so on throughout!

Formatting: Most blog writing platforms come with a ton of formatting options. Use them! Put important points in bold, add quotes, include bullet points etc. All will give your blog some variety for the reader.

VIDEO: CONTENT STANDARDS

Video is now such an accessible medium, and to get started with video you can just use your smartphone. Any phone that has been released in the last couple of years is capable of capturing HD video with a 'workable' sound quality. You can upgrade this with fancy cameras, lighting, microphones, tripods etc. But no matter what kit you have, here are some standards you need to keep an eye on...

Not Looking at the Camera: It sounds obvious, but it's something that a lot of people get wrong. When you use your smartphone, there's a temptation to look at yourself on the screen. Don't do this! Look up at the camera (usually the little black circle at the top) so you're making eye contact with your viewers.

Don't Take Ages Introducing Yourself: It's tempting to do this all the time. But if you've convinced somebody to watch your video, WOW them in the first five seconds! Saying your name ain't gonna do that!

Staying Still: Talking head videos can get boring... quickly. Use different angles, graphics/sound effects/cut-aways to keep attention.

Avoid the Long Intro Sequence: You're not Game of Thrones, you don't need a 90 second title sequence. (If you've already paid somebody on Fiverr to do this for you, sorry... it's gotta go). Any intros should be five seconds max, and come AFTER you've got their attention.

Watch out for the 'Energy Drain Theory': Video sucks personality dry. We've seen the most charismatic people in real life look on video... well... boring! Here's the thing... if you feel like you are giving a 7/10 enthusiasm level whilst recording, it's going to come out as a 4/10. If you want to be super engaging you need to give 15/10 energy levels when recording (this can seem uncomfortable and unnatural), to achieve even an 8/10. We promise this works... try it! You won't look as 'crazy' as you feel!

LIVE VIDEO: CONTENT STANDARDS

Everybody is going LIVE these days! No wonder... it's quick, easy and the social algorithms love it! BUT... you don't want to be 'Going Live' like everybody else, right?

Here's our biggest tip for live video... plan it out.

Treat it like you're doing live TV: know what you're going to say, how long you want to be going live for, and what the purpose is.

There are so many boring live shows, where the presenter spends the first five minutes welcoming people, and the rest of the time stopping mid-sentence to welcome someone else!

Get into the habit of *'recording your live for the replay'*. Chances are you'll get a ton of viewers AFTER you stop streaming… think about them sitting through five minutes of you saying hello to people! B.O.R.I.N.G.

To up your live game, you may want to invest in some software or kit to stream higher quality video from your desktop.

AUDIO: CONTENT STANDARDS

Audio standards are a bit simpler, because there's really only one thing that can go wrong… audio quality.

Basically, if audio is going to be your desired medium YOU MUST INVEST IN A MICROPHONE. There's no excuse for poor audio quality in our opinion.

Don't use a £5 microphone, or a headset you've had since 1994 either.

We aren't saying break the bank on a microphone, but spend what you can afford. If you are broke... don't buy Starbucks for a month and you'll have enough to invest in a microphone.

We bought a Blue Yeti, which was around £100, but Blue also do cheaper models too.

VISUAL: CONTENT STANDARDS

This is the hardest one to fake, so if you don't have a good creative eye, you may want to avoid trying to do this yourself. Find someone who can help you produce something that looks great, if you're prepared to make an investment.

If you ARE a creative, turn it to your advantage. Too many creatives produce average-looking content. C'mon guys, you got this!

If you want to create cool graphics for social media to promote your other content, use something like Canva, which has templates you can steal and is pretty user-friendly. This is ideal if you're not naturally visually creative and it's free to use. Bonus!

HIGHLIGHTING YOUR SKILLS GAPS

If you're new to all this, it may seem a bit overwhelming at first (especially if you opened this book thinking you should be blogging, and have since been convinced otherwise ;))

Don't get overwhelmed.

This is doable.

You can learn this.

You're not the first, you won't be the last.

What do you need to know right now to get started? Make a list of your skills gaps - there is information and people out there to help you actually DO THIS.

(*If you're a member of ATOMIC - post in the group ANYTHING you need help with*)

And remember, you don't have to do it all RIGHT NOW...

CONTENT MVPs & POWER-UPS

Your Content MVP is your 'minimum viable product' for your content. What is the minimum you can start with right now that will get you going at a high enough standard?

Then make a list of Content Power-Ups - things you'd eventually like to add to your content, but you can start without them.

When we first started our YouTube channel, here's what our content MVP and power-ups looked like:

Content MVP:
• HD webcam - attached to Mac
• Blue Yeti microphone
• Learn how to use iMovie
• £30 light

Content Power-Ups:
• Actual camera
• Lapel microphones
• Adobe Premiere/outsource
• Out of office content
• More lighting

Even before this, we just got started using the webcam and microphone on a MacBook Pro, and it was good enough to start with!

CONTENT STAGNATION

The final thing we want you to be wary of before starting your content marketing journey is content stagnation.

This is when your content gets too samey over time, so although you may initially attract an audience with some new, regular content, and ride the buzz over the first few months, you want to ensure you keep their interest, because remember, this is a long-term strategy with short term gains, not a flash in the pan.

We see a lot of content going 'stale' quickly and marketers bring out the classic 'long term strategy' reasoning to excuse their content not working for them.

If it's not getting any sort of reaction, or loses the reaction after the first few months YOU HAVE TO CHANGE IT UP. Something is amiss - don't just let it get worse.

You're allowed to start and get better over time, but you're not allowed to produce the same thing week after week, month after month without improving, innovating and adapting based on the reaction you receive.

Capiche?

KEY TAKEAWAYS FROM MODULE 4: CONTENT CREATION

When creating content, you need to ensure you're creating for your avatar. That might take you down a different path to what you had in mind, but do not worry - all this is doable.

When deciding on a delivery medium, check out the leaders of that medium - see how they are doing it. This will put you head and shoulders above your competition. But also remember you don't have to be 100% there today. In fact, you'll never achieve perfection, so don't kill yourself over it.

To get started with all this, the first thing you need to do is decide on your content MVP - this will get you going. You can add in power-ups at a later date, but there are ways of creating content on-budget at a high enough standard. Find them!

Finally, avoiding content stagnation is important. Be on the lookout for disinterest within your audience and make sure you keep your content fresh!

Once you know what you're creating, the next step is getting it done. The next module outlines the three things you need to have in place to ensure you don't fall behind with your content creation.

MODULE 5:
CONTENT ORGANISATION

Being organised is a vital life skill, not just for content marketing, but for everything! In this module, we're going to help you take all of the overwhelm and panic, and replace them with strategies and processes in place to make it easy for you.

Content organisation (or lack of) is the number one reason why people fail at consistent content creation and marketing – they give up because it's too overwhelming. Our aim with this module is to break everything down for you and make it manageable, habitual and realistic, whilst pushing the boundaries of what you can do.

You'll see why we stressed the importance of mindset back in Module 1, because if you don't prioritise content creation and schedule it into your diary, then it simply won't get done on a regular basis.

You might have all the good intentions in the world, but then one week is particularly busy and you forget, or you had a technical error and it put you off, or you were going to do it but then a client booked you out, or maybe your dog ate your homework! The excuses are endless, and you can feel uninspired to get back into content creation once you fall behind - but excuses are all they are. Once you've got the right processes in place, you'll never slip up again!

Here's the deal:

Organisation... leads to... Consistency... which leads to... Trust... and trust equals... Sales!

So let's get started.

THE BARE MINIMUM

To do the bare minimum of work, you need to be able to answer these three questions:
1. **What** are you going to do?
2. **How** long is it going to take you?
3. **When** are you going to do this?

To help you achieve this, you'll create a Publishing Schedule (What), a Content Task Sheet (How), and a Production Schedule (When).

Using these will allow you to become systematic and habitual in your content creation. In the next module, we'll also look at Content Promotion, which will give us further tasks to add in, so keep that in mind.

PUBLISHING SCHEDULE

This is what people think of when they talk about content plans and calendars. Essentially, it's when you're going to put your stuff out there – when will it be published and when will people be able to read/see/listen to it? Time for you to fill in the answers to these questions:

1. What is the main medium/platform you're going to provide your primary rich content on? This could be YouTube videos, podcast (embedded on blog), SlideDecks on LinkedIn, a Facebook Live show or simply a blog. You must choose only one! You need to nail just one first so you can focus all your energy on it, then you can branch out in the future to do more if you wish

2. How often are you going to put this out? Daily, weekly, fortnightly or monthly? Remember the more regularly you publish content, the more you build your brand equity and the more frequently you can withdraw sales!

3. How can you repurpose your content? Work out how you'll repurpose this to squeeze the most out of what you've created. For instance, you may do a weekly Facebook Live show, that gets syndicated onto a YouTube channel, and a podcast is created from the audio, etc...

Here's a simplified example of a typical publishing schedule:

MON	TUES	WED	THURS	FRI
	Weekly YouTube Video goes live. We email audience to tell them	Facebook Live talking about the same subject as the video from a different perspective	Post the Video on LinkedIn Publisher	Post short teaser clips of the video on all social accounts with a link back to the YouTube video

Remember, all of the hard work is in the initial, rich content that you produce. This is where you spend the most time carrying out research, identifying keywords, writing/filming and editing and so forth. Then all you have to do is distribute and repurpose that across all your platforms.

The important thing to note here is that we don't have to physically create the content on those days, and that's where most people fall down when creating a content plan. They think that if they produce a weekly blog for a Tuesday, that they have to film, edit and publish it all on that Tuesday too, then panic in case they can't manage it.

The purpose of the publishing schedule is solely for when you want things to *appear* online, because you can schedule pretty much everything in advance (apart from the live broadcasts).

Take the opportunity now to plan out a typical week or fortnight, depending on how often you're creating that primary rich content.

Your turn!

Plan a typical day/week/fortnight/month of your publishing schedule goals:

MON	TUES	WED	THURS	FRI

(Feel free to draw this out daily/fortnightly/monthly depending on your publishing schedule)

We rarely recommend only producing one piece of content per month, because that's only 12 items across the entire year – that's not much compared to weekly content, which generates 52 assets per year. Monthly is ok in the beginning, but don't wait too long to start thinking fortnightly and then onto weekly as you get more comfortable. Keep pushing the boundaries.

We started out producing monthly content, but we find now that weekly is EASIER to keep on top of – because it becomes more habitual and gets quicker and easier each week.

Once you've planned your typical week or fortnight, you need to repeat, repeat, repeat! Put it in your diary across the whole year so you know when everything is going to be published.

All of this is a great start, but it's not enough! We want you to be super organised. Knowing when your content is supposed to go out doesn't mean that it actually happens, so we're going to show you how to make sure it does.

CONTENT TASK SHEET

Your publishing schedule is all well and good, but how long is it going to take you to do? When will you fit it in? The Content Task Sheet will help you work out how long it's all going to take you, and whether your publishing schedule is too sparse, or too full.

Look at what you need to publish and break it down into simple small tasks with timings. e.g. based on the previous publishing schedule, this is what your tasks might look like:

TASK	TIME (mins)
Keyword research for video title	20
Information gathering/quote getting/fact finding	30
Script video	40
Record video	40
Edit video	120
Create thumbnail	10
Upload video to YouTube	10
Use Rev.com to add subtitles	10
Save video on external hard drive	5
Tag research and filling in the YouTube description	25
Create a blog on website with video embedded	20
Writing an email to go out to promote it	35
Repurposing tasks:	
Edit together teaser clips and download	25
Choosing three quotes and creating graphics on Canva.com	20
Adding posts to your social media post scheduler	15
Write a draft in LinkedIn Publisher including the new video	5
Post LinkedIn draft on the right day	5
	TOTAL: 435 (7hrs 15mins)

Now it's your turn! Fill in the tasks you will need to complete to achieve your publishing goals (feel free to do this on a separate spreadsheet)

TASK	TIME (mins)
	TOTAL:

In the next part of this module - the 'Production Schedule' - we'll be looking at how you can actually fit all of these weekly tasks into your diary.

You can see in our example that to complete all these tasks would take 7 hours 15 minutes. We have an advantage because there's two of us, and that 7 hours can be brought down as we split up the tasks between us, but for you 7+hrs might be overwhelming. This is also without adding in any of the extra content promotion tasks we mentioned that will be coming up too!

Your total time here needs to be realistic, because if it's way out, you'll become disillusioned trying to complete all of the tasks and never start. If you know you only have 4 hours for content creation a week, then scheduling 7+ hours' worth ain't going to work. Keep it realistic, and if you need more time, then work smarter! Here are some tips:

Delegate

YOU DON'T HAVE TO DO IT ALL YOURSELF!

We'll be honest here, we're perfectionists and found it very hard to let go of tasks we know we can nail. But with the amount of content we wanted to produce, we needed to start outsourcing.

We dabbled in outsourcing tasks and it was going well, but the one thing we could never let go of was our video editing! Video editing was our baby, like seriously, who else could do it like us? Who else could get our sense of humour and energy and make sure to leave in the right funny outtakes? Nobody!

After 50 videos, the videos had proven themselves successful and were generating us money. The more we published, the more our audience grew, and the more sales we made. Great. BUT the editing was becoming a burden, the style we were going for was extremely time-consuming because we were 'jump-cutting' and adding lots of effects and graphics. It was taking us around 3-4 hours all in all. We had to do something about it!

Luckily, a lady called Christina Fleming was recommended to us. We had a meeting, she seemed legit, and we sent her our raw footage of our upcoming video... when we got it back we were blown away - she totally kicked our editing ass! It was so much better than our editing: slicker, better graphics and sound effects etc. She totally 'got' us. We posted it and immediately the retention rate on that video and for future videos has been almost 20-30% higher than when we were doing it! Yikes!

Now we have three hours back in our life each week where we can produce even more content... or just go home early ;)

The funny thing is, Christina can edit twice as well in half the time - making it a no-brainer for us. The time we save is more than worth the investment we pay Christina. It also meant we could start batching our recordings a little more and start saving a ton of time, allowing us to put more effort into more revenue-generating activities - so we started making MORE money!

At first it may seem scary to outsource, but once you've proven your content is working, outsourcing isn't a cost, it's an opportunity to make more money!

Have a think about what's taking you the longest and who you can get to do it for you instead.

Automate

We use tools for everything! We swear that we do the work of 12 people between us just by using extra tools.

Tools like SmarterQueue, Zapier, ConvertKit and Rev are some of our faves but there are too many to mention in detail. Put it this way, if you're doing a task that takes ages, there's probably a tool for that! And if there is, spending a few quid/dollars a month to save you hours of time is probably worth it!

Keep following our YouTube channel as we always like to feature new timesaving tools :)

Necessities vs. Desirables

Establish which of the tasks you've identified are your *necessities*, and which are your desirables. For us, our necessities are getting the YouTube video done, putting it on our blog, and sending out the promo email. Every single week, we HAVE to achieve our *necessities*, so even if we're pushed for time, we absolutely make sure we complete them as the bare necessities that we want to do. No matter how busy we are, we prioritise these tasks every week.

Everything else are your *desirables*. You **should be able to manage everything** each and every week, but if you're exceptionally busy or ill or whatever one week, you can skip out on the desirables. e.g. for us, making additional graphics, LinkedIn Publisher, live video and

Instagram stories are desirables only, we'll do them each week unless we're behind on time.

To save time take a look now at your content tasks and divide them up into one of these four areas:

DO MYSELF (THE NECESSITIES)	DITCH (THE DESIRABLES)	OUTSOURCE	AUTOMATE
What's essential for you to do and doesn't make sense delegating?	What's the 'nice to do' if you have time?	What can you outsource to save you a ton of time?	What can you put on automate with the right tools?

If you want to do it all and can't outsource or delegate any more, then just simply give yourself more time. Rather than weekly videos, they could be shared every two weeks instead, or even monthly. That way, the 7+hours a week only becomes 3.5 hours a week or less. Eventually you can start to increase the frequency again.

Now you've got your content task sheet, you need to turn this into a production schedule.

PRODUCTION SCHEDULE

This is the part people struggle with, but not you! We see it time and time again, people committing to weekly content being published without a clue of WHEN that's actually going to get created each week. If it's not in the diary then it won't get done - simple as that.

The key is to have a regular time slot in your diary each week to produce all your content. It might be on a Wednesday afternoon or a Friday morning; for us though, that's a Tuesday. EVERY Tuesday! You can't even hire us on a Tuesday, we'll turn you down, because it's our content day and nothing can be booked in otherwise. You might think that's crazy, but we know that more content = more money, and we've never lost a client due to having this discipline. We have occasionally swapped the Tuesday for another day for speaking gigs etc, but it's rare.

It's time to give yourself a time slot and be disciplined enough to stick to it!

Periodically vs. Batching

There are two ways to create your production schedule: the first is periodically, whether that's weekly, fortnightly or monthly, i.e. you create a video each week.

The second is batching plus periodic tasks (because you can't always batch everything) where you produce all your content in one go i.e. you create 10 videos in one go to be released as and when.

Pros of Periodically:

You Improve Over Time - When doing *periodical* production, you can constantly, and vastly, improve on each piece of content you create. We'd highly recommend periodical production for those who are new to creating content (blogging, videos, podcasting) because you will get better and better after reviewing each one. There will come a time when you plateau at your performance level and that's when it's good to start batching.

Reactive - You can quickly create something based on what is trending right now or what is fresh in your industry, and publish it as soon as possible - rather than having to wait months for your batch of videos to go out.

Smaller Time Chunks - You can start right now, you don't have to free up a whole day or more to produce a ton of content in one go!

Pros of Batching:

Time efficient - It's much more productive to batch your content creation and overall you will save time.

No Weekly Worry - If batching, you will need to block out large chunks of time to create all this content, but after that you don't need to worry about it.

Cost Reduction - If you're batching and outsourcing elements of your content tasks then it can often be much cheaper to do this in batches too.

With batching, there will still be a need for some additional periodic tasks, but nowhere near as many.

There are pros and cons to each, so pick the method you think would work best for you. If you're just starting out or you're trying out some new styles of content, then it may be best to start off periodically, before moving to batching.

We talked earlier in the book about establishing your content stamp, and this involves trying out new ideas and seeing what reaction you get to the different types of content you are producing. There's no point in batch-making 20 videos, for example, if you don't even know they will get a good reaction.

The Periodic Production Schedule

With the *periodic* production schedule, you create content as you go based on your content task sheet.

Let's continue to use the earlier example. The content task sheet says

1 piece of content (including repurposing) = 7.5 hours' worth of work

If we're publishing **weekly**, we therefore need to find 7.5 **hours** per week.

Similarly, ...

If we're publishing **fortnightly**, we need to find 7.5 hours per **fortnight**

If we're publishing **monthly**, we need to find 7.5 hours per **month**

Weekly publishing lends itself to a weekly production schedule, but if you're publishing monthly you may want to break that 7.5 hours down across multiple days in the month if you wish.

Batching Production Schedule

With the batching production schedule, you're doing more content creation in one go.

Not everything is going to be able to be batched, so there is stuff you will still be doing periodically.

*Let's look at an example of a weekly **publishing** schedule, with a batched **production** schedule.*

From the content task sheet, we know that one piece of content takes 7.5 hours to complete, but out of that we can:

Batch Produce = **5 hours**
Weekly Produce = **2.5 hours**

The first step is deciding how much we wish to batch in one go. Let's say we do six pieces of content.

6 x 5 Hours = 30 hours

So we need to schedule in 30 hours (3.5 days approx.) every six weeks for our content creation, with 2.5 hours also scheduled in each week.

With batching, we can often do things quicker in bulk, so that 30 hours may be significantly less. Time yourself on your first go, to see realistically how much time you need to batch.

Put it in Your Calendar

Whether you decide to go with a periodic or batched schedule, you will have time that needs to be allotted to tasks. To make this an actual production schedule, mark off this time in your diary and treat it like a meeting.

Using Project Days for Upskilling

At Andrew and Pete, we have what we call *project days* most Mondays and Fridays, which is when we focus on business development. It's when we work on our own business doing things like: integrating time saving tools, learning how to create videos and do the editing, implementing a new ad strategy, implementing messenger bots, writing our latest book and so on...

You may need to also book out some time separately to your weekly schedule to work on things like this too. For example, if you need to learn how to edit videos, do that in a project day, not your weekly content time! Otherwise you will just use up all of your valuable content creation time faffing on learning video editing. Don't mix up the two and use up your time. There needs to be discipline when it comes to your content creation time slot.

Discipline

It sounds cheesy, but every second HAS to count. Curiosity didn't kill the cat... procrastination did.

This is why you need discipline, and respect for your time. When you're in your content creation time, nothing else should be distracting to you, your phone should be out of sight and out of mind on silent, do not disturb mode should be switched on on your computer, and you need a passive aggressive sign on your door so nobody dares knock.

The reason we assign time limits when producing the content task sheet isn't just to make sure we know how long everything is going to take us, it's because of Parkinson's Law: time expands to fit the task at hand. We know we have 30 minutes to script a video, so we never go over that. We set a timer and make sure we finish in that half an hour. Assign time limits and stick to them.

We've become pretty efficient with managing our time, to the point where we know exactly what we're doing every day for the next three months and beyond. You don't need to be as efficient and organised as us yet; it's something we've learned over time, and we've got better at it as we've gone along.

We look at people more organised than we are, and try to replicate their systems and processes for our business. This is what we want for you: "Start small, progress fast." You have the potential to achieve the same amount of content as we have. Start with the bare minimum – what are you publishing, how long will it take you, and when will you fit it in?

KEY TAKEAWAYS FROM MODULE 5: CONTENT ORGANISATION

Half of the battle of content marketing is just simply keeping up with creating content. By breaking it down and scheduling it in your diary, you'll find that it becomes a habit, and before you know it, you will have been consistently publishing content for six months, a year, two years... forever.

Remember all you need is a publishing schedule (*what* you're publishing), a content task sheet (*how* long is going to take), and a production schedule (*when* it is scheduled in to do).

Once you've figured out your content stamp and are consistently creating content that people like, the next step is to plan strategically how to promote it. The next module outlines what you need to do in the most efficient and cost-effective way.

MODULE 6:

CONTENT PROMOTION

There's no point in promoting crap content!

Promotion is the sexy part of content marketing that everybody reads about – the email campaigns, SEO, Facebook Ads, social media etc. But before you get started, it's important to lay all the groundwork that we talked about in the preceding modules. When you're comfortable and familiar with your content stamp and are organised with your content production, you're then ready to look at maxing out all avenues of promoting your content. **Not** before.

Obviously, before now you will have been promoting your content, but this module is all about creating a more formal strategy to get your content out there in the most cost-effective way.

We want you to find the right path for your business, so we'll outline the various methods for driving traffic and you can figure out what's right for you to focus on.

THE AVENUES FOR CONTENT PROMOTION

There are hundreds and thousands of ways to promote your content but they mainly all boil down into three main avenues you can focus on: Search, Social and Email. Within each of these, there are a range of options to choose from.

Multiple books dedicated to each of these avenues still wouldn't be enough to cover everything, and they would be outdated pretty quickly too, so we're going to give you our best tips on deciding which avenues are going to be best for you. From there it's up to you to keep yourself in the know and up to date with the best promotion strategies in those avenues.

This is why we promote continuous learning over on our membership site ATOMIC (www.andrewandpete.com/atomic), where there are weekly trainings and community support. So if you want to learn more and deep dive into the different promotional avenues, go join ATOMIC! :)

Let's dive in!

SEARCH ENGINE OPTIMISATION (SEO)

This is the process of ranking for specific search terms that your target audience is looking for on search engines such as Google or Bing. It's kind of seen as the holy grail to be on page one of Google, because the idea is you can sit back and relax without spending any money and thousands of visitors will come to your site and buy your stuff while you sip piña coladas on the beach.

We've all been sold this dream, and you wouldn't believe how many businesses come to us asking to be on page one of Google within the next week - as if we can just click our fingers and they will be there!

It's not quite as simple as that unfortunately. It is possible, but it takes hard work, being clever, and a bit of patience.

There's a myth that SEO is technical and overly complicated, but don't worry – it's not really a 'dark art' and you CAN master it.

Getting a Page to Rank on Google

If SEO is going to be a main strategy for driving traffic, then there's no point in writing blogs willy nilly and hoping that they'll rank. You need to be smarter about it.

So how do you do that? The first thing is understanding Domain Authority (DA). DA is basically a mark out of 100 that Google gives your website based on a number of factors. Thus, when deciding whose website should be in what position on Google, it looks to see if your DA is higher than a competitor's DA.

This is the same for individual pages and blogs too, not just your site overall. So for example, a blog on your website (depending on the quality and how popular that blog is) will have a similar mark out of 100 - this is called Page Authority. Your page will rank higher than another page with a lower page authority score within relevant keyword searches.

Start to get smart about which blogs you can write that have a chance of ranking on page one of Google. After all, there's really no point in ranking on page three of Google, right?!

By using a tool called MozBar, you can actually see what page authority other blogs have on page one of Google BEFORE you even start writing. If you have a DA of 20, and page one of Google is filled with websites that have a DA of 40+, then it's unlikely you'll stand a chance of ranking for that term. But if all the sites on page one have a DA of 10-20, you've got a shot.

Essentially, you should know if you can rank for a keyword search term BEFORE you even write it. This is why we said you need to be smart. Most people think of a topic they can write about and then try to make it rank in search - whereas in reality this is just a waste of time IF your main strategy is SEO. There are of course other ways to get traffic, but just don't be expecting it to rank because you stuffed it with keywords.

The smarter way to spend your time writing blogs is to figure out what blog topics you can rank for FIRST and then write those blogs instead! It takes more time to research of course, but we'd much rather write 10 blogs that get a ton of traffic, as opposed to a hundred blogs that don't get anything. (Again, ATOMIC members can get a full in-depth step by step guide on how to do this, it's called 'Blogging for Page 1').

For some industries, this is harder or easier. Industries like travel, insurance and marketing are extremely competitive and trying to rank for anything in these industries can be tough! Other industries like funeral directors and accountants can often be a lot easier as they are usually more localised services. You are competing more against others in your area, rather than the whole world.

The important thing to note is that you can build your domain authority over time, which will allow you to rank for more competitive terms. If you're just starting out, your DA is likely to be less than 10. If you've been producing content on your site for years and have been doing some guest blogs with links back to your site, you might be looking at a score around the 20-40 mark. Bigger news sites are around 70-90, and sites like Facebook have 100/100!

To check your own domain authority, just go to: www.moz.com/researchtools/ose/ where you can type in your own domain (or anyone else's) and find out your score. You get three daily searches for free.

What you may find is that your DA isn't as high as you'd like, and that you're going to find it tough to find keywords that you can rank for. So if you just don't have the resources to spend on SEO, sometimes search isn't the right promotional avenue for you just yet.

In the meantime, however, don't just simply forget about it - keep a little checklist of small things you can be doing that over time will make a big impact on your DA. For example:

- Writing more content around your niche and certain topics that you want to be found for. This is called a Content Hub, whereby you have lots of blogs written around focussed keywords that interlink and complement each other
- Constantly linking back to other blogs you have written. When you've written a blog, why not go back to previous blogs and link them to your latest blog too?
- Guest blogging on other sites for a link back to your own. A link back to your site from a website with a high DA will help you more
- Registering your site on industry directories is often a good place to start
- Making sure your 'Google Webmasters' and 'Google my Business' profiles are up to date
- Making sure your website is running as fast as possible and is mobile friendly
- We could go on all day...

Another massive factor when it comes to search is simply making the best possible content around that keyword. For example, our good friend Ian Anderson

Gray from Seriously Social wrote a blog all about how to go Live on Facebook from your desktop (at the time when you could only go Live from your mobile).

The blog was so incredibly in-depth and helpful that everyone loved it, commented on it and shared it - including some influential people. Each of these things gives Google extremely strong signals that this blog is helpful and thus is more likely to give the blog a high page authority and rank it higher up in the search results for this keyword. The blog has generated over 1,300 comments, 21.8k shares and gets around 100,000 visits a month. How insane! It actually brought down his site temporarily because it couldn't even handle so much traffic.

Again, this is why we stress the importance of creating great content. The more engaging it is, the better chance you have of ranking in search. For Ian, this is exactly what he did. He made an incredibly in-depth article that was so helpful and engaging that it got a ton of comments and shares and in return Google ranked the blog on page one.

As a result of this, Ian was able to generate thousands of subscribers just from this one blog alone, as people opted in to one of his website pop-ups. Furthermore, he was able to successfully launch his Facebook Live OBS and Wirecast courses off the back of this highly targeted database.

This is search done perfectly. Hats off to you Ian!

Hopefully by now you can see how search works in relation to the Andrew and Pete's Content Model. By providing relevant and engaging primary rich content for a keyword we can rank for, we start to draw in traffic to the top of our funnel.

So what do you think? Is it worth focussing on right now, or is it something you want to keep building up to?

Let's have a look at the next promotional avenue for distributing your content.

SOCIAL MEDIA MARKETING

Using social media platforms to build a following and send traffic back to your website is a proven, popular and largely free way to promote your content. It's our favourite distribution method, yet we see so many people do it horrifically wrong.

The idea of social media marketing is to get discovered, build relationships and then to ultimately drive lead generation. That's the overall idea and it sounds so simple... but the intricacies are not.

There are three things you need to master with social media marketing and they are, 'Social', 'Media', and 'Marketing' haha!

But first, let's tackle the one thing everyone struggles with: **which platform should you focus on?!**

The temptation is to be on all the platforms, and if you have the resources to do that then great - go for it! However, we believe that most smaller businesses and solopreneurs just simply don't have enough time or manpower for that. If you're trying to be everywhere at once, you're going to be nowhere all at once!

If you're trying to juggle them all you will be spreading your efforts too thinly and you won't be making the progress you deserve. You'll end up playing social media Twister... left foot on Twitter, right hand on YouTube, right foot on Pinterest, left hand on Faceb-Oooops you've fallen over!

Wouldn't you much rather have 10,000 followers on one platform than 100 followers on every platform known to man?

Once you've built up your following on one platform with a solid focus, consistent posting, and the nurturing of your fans, it's easier to move people over to another platform you want to grow.

By all means feel free to grab the usernames for your business on the other platforms, but fight the temptation to be on all of them. Choose one or two to concentrate on with one definitive, dominant platform to master and nurture.

Choose the platform where your target market hangs out but also the platform that best suits the type of content you want to create for your content stamp.

Once you've done this, let's start getting strategic.

Social

The world of social media is full of people just linking to their sales pages and setting auto-DMs - pretty much everything is scheduled or automated and people are getting sick of it. In fact, recent trends suggest that the algorithms are trying to punish this behaviour, because what we all seem to be forgetting is the SOCIAL part of social media.

We get that it's tough to keep up, and automation and scheduling allows you to show up without it being a time drain - BUT you can't forget about being social. If you're never on the platform talking to people, how are you supposed to ever build meaningful relationships?

This is the part of social media that you can't put an ROI value on - relationships. How can you measure a conversation that might one day lead to a sale years later, or talking to someone who isn't even in your target market who goes on to introduce you to your dream client... you can't place a value on that and you can't measure it. The one thing we do know is that by taking the time to talk to people you start to build trust and fans who will share your content, tell others about you and ultimately buy from you.

At the end of the day, the more conversations you have, the more sales you will get.

Moreover, having conversations with someone increases the amount of time they spend engaging with your profile. This gives a strong indication to social media algorithms that this person likes you and will want to see more of your posts in the future. So having conversations with people means the algorithms are more likely to show that person your future content. Boom! To reiterate:

The more conversations you have, the more reach you get!

How about that!

So how do you go about having more conversations? Try to be proactive. Don't just rely on people coming to you first. The more you comment on others' content, the more likely they are to comment on yours and come check you out. The more you reach out first, the more conversations you have and the more people get drawn in to you.

On platforms like Twitter this is easy because you probably follow your potential customers or have them in a Twitter list - and so it's easy to just scroll through the timeline and comment on people's posts and ask questions.

This is much harder on Facebook but it still works the same. You can still go to other pages and groups, or even personal profiles and interact with others' posts proactively.

If someone comments on your content, do you just say thank you? Or do you ask them follow up questions and get to know them?

Do you just reply with text, or do you respond with a video?

Do you reach out in private messenger/DMs and continue the conversations?

Do you tag them in posts that are relevant to them?

Do you share their content?

All these things help you to build meaningful relationships that set you apart from everyone else on social media. Is it time you were more social on social?

Media

Now you know the power of being more social, you do need to give people a reason to follow you in the first place and build up some credibility.

The idea here is that by posting useful content around your niche, you start to paint the picture that you are an expert.

If you're talking about 'XYZ' all the time, it makes sense that others would start to trust you know all about 'XYZ' and keep following you. So that's what you need to be doing: posting as much content as you can around your niche to build up some brand equity.

The issue here is that many people post other people's content more than their own.

People seem to think that if you want more visibility on social, then you should just post more. The problem is you probably don't have enough content to post more, so then what you end up doing is posting links to other people's articles and news.

This is fine to a degree, after all it's content around your expertise, but put it this way: **it's not building your brand equity - it's building theirs!**

Every time you post other people's content you're basically building their brand equity and not yours, so it's not really all that useful to you.

Yes, you are getting some more visibility each time you post, and yes people appreciate good curation of valuable content, but you're not getting all the credit. Wouldn't it be better if you were posting more of your own content and getting all the credit?!

So that's what we want you to do, post more of your own primary content. Post links back to your primary rich content on your website (or wherever it maybe be) and also find ways to repurpose your primary rich content into smaller chunks of primary content that you can post.

By repurposing your content, you can quickly turn one rich piece of content into dozens of smaller chunks that help you fill up your social media timeline.

e.g. One video on YouTube could be turned into a blog, the audio from the video could become a podcast or soundbite, the tips from the video could be read out via Facebook Live Audio, the tips could be turned into graphics and quotes, you could make an infographic from the stats, you could create a teaser video or a fun outtakes video... it's endless!

Essentially you are taking your primary rich content and making the most of it by repurposing it to make it work on your preferred social platforms.

By making content specifically for the specific platform you're dominant on, you have a greater chance of that content performing better.
Essentially, it's engaging content native to that platform that always wins. Even if this means posting more engaging content LESS frequently because of time restraints.

If you decided your primary rich content was designed specifically for a certain platform, i.e. YouTube Channel or Facebook Live Show... always make sure this goes on your blog too. Remember you want to be building your domain authority on your website and making sure when people visit your site they can lose themselves in your content.

Marketing

It's all well and good to post great, engaging content and build a following of meaningful relationships, but you're a business - and businesses need to make money! So how do you turn this following into cash?! Well, that's all to do with secondary content.

If you have a physical product that you sell, it can be quite easy to just showcase your product in fun ways, e.g. using images, GIFs, videos, user-generated content and so on... but for service providers it can be quite hard.

Either way, in addition to the primary content that you are posting to make people feel happier or smarter, you also want to be posting about your offering. The ratio here should be around 80% primary and 20% secondary.

For us, we don't post about our services all that much on social, but what we do post regularly are opportunities to get people subscribed to our email list. Whether that's a link to register for our upcoming webinar, for our weekly vlogs, or for a specific lead magnet (a lead magnet is when you offer some bonus content in return for an email address, e.g. download this free eBook on 'XYZ'...)

Social media is a place for being social, not for aggressive sales. Offering something for free is a much softer sell, and once on your email list and in your sales funnel, you can be more direct with the sales.

Having conversations with people does often open up opportunities to sell (only if they ask first), but offering different lead magnets is a much more scalable way to grow your sales on social media.

We're going to be talking more about how secondary content comes into play in the next and final module, but on the subject of email...

EMAIL MARKETING

Email Marketing is our first love when it comes to marketing and it should be yours too! It holds the power to sell what you want, whenever you want.

We get most of our sales from our email because it's highly engaged and targeted, and we're going to show you how to do the same.

It's important to get people signed up your email list because that data is yours. When it comes to your social following, you never know when people will lose interest in the platform, or when your page might get taken down with no warning etc. But email is much safer. Emails can be backed up, and people skip breakfast more often than they do email!

Email is also a much more acceptable place to openly sell, and so the general sales funnel we take is:

1. Build a social following
2. Get people to subscribe to our email
3. Use email to sell our products

That's the route most marketers will tell you to go, but there's a step missing here!

After you get their email address, you need to keep building your brand equity first, and THEN you can sell to them....

1. Build a social following
2. Get people to subscribe to your email
3. **Build brand equity with your email list**
4. Use email to sell your products

The good news is that the effort to keep building your equity is fairly low, as you can use the content you're already creating.

For example, we have a weekly vlog that we create for YouTube which then gets emailed out to our email subscribers each week. We don't create more content just for our emails, we don't send people boring updates or company news, we just send them our primary rich content.

It's that subscriber loop we mentioned earlier. People subscribe and get sent more content that builds our brand equity. Each week our whole audience gets to see us talking about marketing and over time they start to A) come to realise that we know our stuff and, B) start to really like us for being so helpful and entertaining. In the meantime - we're getting more views on our content - yippee!

After you've sent out a number of valuable emails, say four or five, you're then at the point where you've built up enough trust and credibility so that you can take a withdrawal of all that brand equity you've built, i.e. sell something!

Selling AFTER building your equity means your emails will have higher open rates, higher click through rates, and generate more sales!!

Our email open rates are 2-3x that of the industry average just because we do it this way. It's extremely effective.

It doesn't have to be a set ratio of one sales email after every four useful emails either. It depends on how strong your content is, how often you send emails and if it's a hard or soft sell.

We find one every four or five works well for us, and funnily enough we get an extremely low percentage of unsubscribes whenever we send our sales emails, because we have EARNED it and people respect them.

However, the more content you create, the more brand equity you build and thus the more opportunities you have to sell. So if you were to sell every four emails, and you only have a monthly newsletter - that's one sales email every four months!

Yikes! Weekly emails for us means that we get to sell every month without annoying people, or looking spammy!

Just sit and take that in for a moment, because there's no greater incentive to creating your best content more frequently. **The more frequently you email primary content, the more opportunities you have to sell.** The people who send daily emails or have a daily podcast are giving themselves extra chances to sell to their audience, because they're giving immense value all the time.

We should note here that regular emails are not the same as spamming. If you're sharing useful content that people want, and you're making them happier or smarter, they're not going to feel spammed. Rather, they'll welcome your emails.

It doesn't take us long to write weekly emails either because we're just simply sending them a link to our vlog. We used to do monthly newsletters but there was always so much to fit in that it would take us ages to write. It's actually QUICKER for us to send weekly emails than it was to send monthly emails!!! Go figure.

Moreover, because each email only has one call to action at a time, the click-through rates (how many people actually click a link in your email) are vastly better. So there's another tip - make sure each email has only one Call to Action - it's either sending them some helpful primary content or it's selling something. Too many different calls to action decreases the likelihood of someone clicking on either!

Final point, **don't call your newsletter a 'newsletter'!** The word 'newsletter' sounds synonymous with 'spam' and also 'borrrrring'!

Try to brand it up almost like a free product, for example, ours is called Atomic Lite and we send you weekly short, fun, training videos on how to kick ass at content marketing! Sounds good, right?! Our friends at Orbit Media call theirs 'The Orbiter'. It's your chance to get creative!

If you want to know more about how to create lead magnets, landing pages, the best software to use, which is the best email service provider, how to set up a welcome series, and how to use ads to get people subscribed - then you can get all this info on ATOMIC.

PROMOTION POWER UPS

Content marketing relies on these three avenues (search, social, email) to promote content, but for the impatient ones amongst you, you might find that these methods aren't happening as fast as you need/want them to. It takes time to cultivate and grow your social media following, it takes time to get lots of ranking articles on search and it takes time to build your email funnels and get people subscribing. Sooooo, here are three ways you can POWER UP these avenues to get quicker results!

This is the next level, power booster pack which will get you further, faster.

Paid

You can pay to get more traffic to your content, and there's nothing wrong with paying for what you don't have yet. If you don't have a large email list, or you're just starting out on social media and want to boost your results, don't be afraid to pay to get there faster.

The easiest example (although not necessarily the best) is the 'boost' button on Facebook – every time you create a post, you'll see a 'Boost' button, where for a few pounds you can get your post in front of a lot more people.

There are also Facebook Ads (much more effective than boosting btw), Google AdWords, Twitter Ads, Promoted Pins, YouTube Ads, and so on, for you to promote your content with.

There are also outreach services like Outbrain, which charge you for promoting your content on other sites. It simply displays your content and you pay every time someone clicks on it.

Should you pay to promote every bit of content? Probably not! There are only two times when you should pay to promote your content:

1. Maximise well-performing content: If a piece of content starts doing super well, people start engaging with it or it gets picked up by a third party and goes slightly viral, then put some money behind it to get it seen by more people. Facebook will even notify you when one post is outperforming all the others. If people are engaging with it, make the most of it.

2. When it's part of a strategic lead gen. promotion: When you create content specifically to get people subscribed and into your funnel, of course pay to get more reach to that type of content too.

Collaboration

If you want to get your content to a wider audience of your target market, and do so in the quickest, cheapest and most effective way, you should collaborate with others.

If you're collaborating with people who have a big audience, and they share your collaboration with their audience, you are going to grow extremely fast indeed.

Collaboration should be win-win all round, with everybody getting more exposure to each other's audiences.

So every time we collaborate, we are growing in credibility, getting exposed to more people, growing our audience, learning more, and saving ourselves some time in the process! Boom!

This is also why we love being guests on other people's shows - because we are exposed to people not already in our audience. It's definitely the quickest free way to grow your audience in our opinion.

Don't worry about collaborating with your 'competition' too. It's extremely short-sighted to think that by collaborating with your competitor you are going to lose business. In most industries, there's enough room for everyone, and we've found that having good relationships with people who do what we do has only been beneficial to our own growth.

Don't just wait for people to reach out to you to collaborate either - be proactive, ask people to be guests on your show, or to be a guest on their show. Think about who you can work with, starting with your peers, and create a dream list of collaborators. Actively seek out potential collaborators and start building relationships now. Keep in mind the value you bring - you need to bring something new to the table for their audience. Don't reach out selfishly!

Sharing

This could sound a bit airy-fairy, but it isn't - please don't underestimate shareability.

To give yourself the best chance, go back to Module 3 and start thinking of content ideas that get people sharing!

Here are some other tips to get people sharing on social media specifically:

Tag a mate: By asking people to tag a friend, it gets them to actively share your content to their audience, as well as increasing comments (things the algorithms love).

Share if you learn: Challenge people to share your post if they learn something! This works a treat.

Ask for the shares: Just directly ask viewers/readers to like, comment and share your content. If you ask, people are more likely to do it.

Sneak and Tag Collab: This is a cool one! If you use any examples or case studies in your blog and mention any businesses or brand specifically in a favourable light... tag them on social media or reach out to them and let them know you've mentioned them. Chances are - they'll share it too! Be careful not to look disingenuous - don't just mention them in the hopes for a share, do it for the right reasons.

Ask your friends: If you're particularly proud of a piece of content, simply ask your connections to share it! When we first contributed to Social Media Examiner (an online news and resource for businesses using social media) we asked 10 of our closest friends to help us get the ball rolling and get the word out there. People are roughly 32x more likely to share your content if it's been shared by others already!

Blast out groups: We've also been involved in blast-out groups in the past, which can work well. This is where you have a few people with a shared or related audience and you host a private group online. Whenever one of the members has published something or has something new to talk about, they post it in the blast-out group and everyone else shares, comments or likes it. This is a great way to mutually help and grow each other's audiences. Why not set up a blast out group yourself?

ORGANISING YOUR PROMOTIONAL TASKS

Now it's time to add all of your promotional activities to your content task sheet.

Decide what you're going to be doing each week, how long it will take to complete the tasks, and add them to your production schedule. The same applies for SEO, social and email, paid promotion, collaboration and shareability.

Once it's all scheduled in, you can now feel confident about what content is getting published, how it's being promoted and when it's all going to get done.

KEY TAKEAWAYS FROM MODULE 6: CONTENT PROMOTION

Content promotion can seem like an endless stream of things to do. The key is being strategic and sensible, and relying on a few main ways to get traffic to your content.

Decide upon a promotional mix based on search, social and email - where are you focussing your efforts (at least for the time being), and what needs to be added to your content production schedule to ensure consistency?

Also decide if any of the promotion power-ups are right for you, and what steps need to be taken to get those rockin'.

In the next module, we look at how this newly built audience is going to be turned into leads and sales!

MODULE 7:

CONTENT LEAD GENERATION

First things first, congratulations for making it this far (especially to those of you who have been actioning this as we go). In this final module, we talk SALES!

At this point you should:

- Know what makes your business remarkable and how to describe that
- Have crafted an awesome brand that is going to allow you to make better decisions and come up with creative ideas
- Know exactly who you are creating content for to build an audience of potential customers - and be building brand equity in each and every one!
- Have created a content stamp - that's going to make this process all the easier, as you'll have a unique way to spread your message
- Within your content stamp you should know your content delivery medium that suits your avatar

- You should have your content MVP ready to start creating...
- ... and a content task sheet, production schedule and publishing schedule to keep you in check
- PLUS a banging promo plan that's going to get your content in front of as many people as possible

If you do all of the above, you'll be absolutely rocking it online, building TRUST and ATTENTION with the right sorts of people, building an audience of followers who love what you do, developing authority, credibility and respect in your field, and all that's left to do is...

...turn that into sales!

Let's not beat around the bush here either. There are tons of reasons you may want to be producing content:

- To genuinely help people
- To gain respect of your peers
- Because you actually enjoy it
- To self-improve
- To document what you're learning
- To go viral on FB, and end up on Big Brother

But the one thing we all have in common is:

- To grow our businesses

And that requires SALES.

Some people are put off asking for a sale. You may not want to appear salesy, slimy or disingenuous. You may be frightened of getting a NO. You may wonder what people will think of you.

But selling your stuff is not a bad thing.

Unless you have a crap product/service that is ripping people off and you know it, you should never feel ashamed about selling.

Selling HELPS people. You have a solution to their problem, and it is YOUR DUTY to let them know about it!

So let's not look at 'sales' as a dirty word. In fact, let's unite sales and marketing departments - there is far too much separation here, when in fact, nowadays they are more and more one and the same thing.

In this module we are going to show you how to sell with content marketing in a way that is comfortable and effective!

BACK TO THE CONTENT MODEL

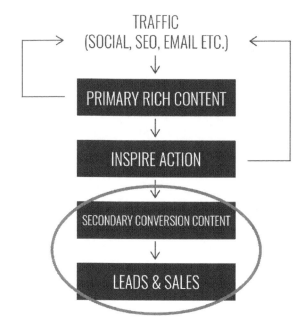

Remember Andrew and Pete's Content Model from back in Module 1? Up until now, we have focussed on the top half of it - where we are publishing primary content and using the subscriber loop to keep our audience engaged.

Now we're moving down the model and we are going to use two types of secondary content to generate leads and sales.

HAND RAISERS AND GATED CONTENT

The key to Content Lead Generation is what we call *'hand raisers.'*

Basically, we have built this audience, and now we need a way to work out WHO in our audience is *readier* to buy than the rest, by getting them to metaphorically *raise their hand.*

Question: So, how do you get these metaphorical 'hand raisers'?
Answer: By creating 'Gated Secondary Content'.

Gated content is a type of content that requires some form of opt-in to receive the content (the classic being 'give me an email address and I'll give you it', though there are other ways we're going to talk about). Basically, you need to know WHO has accessed your content for it to be considered 'gated'.

Secondary content, remember, is content designed to sell your product or service. It should be all about you, what you do, and how bloomin' awesome you are.

Therefore, **gated secondary content** is both about your product/service AND requires some way of knowing who has accessed it. Do you see how this creates hand raisers? If you know who in your audience wants more information about buying from you, then you know their interest is at least piqued!

We're going to talk about the ways to gate content in a moment, but first let's look at what type of content should and shouldn't be gated.

What Should and Shouldn't be Gated?

Don't Gate: Primary rich content. Any content that falls under your content stamp you want to keep free and accessible to all... forever! You may be asking people to subscribe to this content, but they should be able to access it no matter if they subscribe or not. It should be freely available and easy to find online. They might be interested in the content, but it doesn't necessarily mean they want to buy from you.

Gate: Secondary conversion content which shows some *potential* to buy. Things like webinars, price-guides, eBooks, reports, get on the waiting list, see a demo etc.

Accessing this content doesn't necessarily need to mean the person is eager to hand over their money, we're just looking to find out who might be warmer in our audience than others.

Don't Gate: 'Convince to Buy' secondary content. Things like testimonials, awards, reviews, FAQs etc. Content that paints your business in a good light should be freely accessible for all to see. We're going to talk about how this type of content comes into play later on in this module.

HOW TO GATE YOUR CONTENT

We've traditionally talked about the four ways to gate content and get hand raisers, but at the time of writing a bonus fifth way is emerging.

Let's look at the original four first.

1. Email Address Unlocks Content: This is what most people think of when they hear 'gated content'. In order to access content, you have to give a correct email address and the content is sent to you. This could be a PDF, a webinar, video series, or the content could simply be delivered within the email itself.

2. Information Ask: Another way you can gate content is by asking people for information before you can deliver the content. A good example of this is 'Request a Quote' - you need to know certain parameters before you can give them the suitable content.

In both these examples, the person knows they are accessing gated content, BUT that doesn't always have to be the case...

3. **Email Tagging**: If you've already got their email address, you can release secondary content to your list. The beauty of this is that to access it, all somebody has to do is click! Most Email Service Providers (ESP) will allow you to create subsets of your list based on actions subscribers take. In our ESP this is called 'tagging' (it may have a different terminology in yours). You can tag people on your list who have accessed specific content you've sent them via email, thus allowing you to follow up on that subset.

4. Facebook Custom Audiences: This breaks one rule of gated content, in that you don't actually know who has accessed the content, but Facebook will allow you to create custom audiences of people who have watched or read specific types of content. You don't know who is in the audience but you do know how many, and you can serve follow-up ads to these people.

You can create custom audiences based on which pages of your website people have visited (via the Facebook Pixel), or on how they've engaged with your content on your Facebook and Instagram page (for example you can create an audience of people who have watched 50% of a secondary content video).

And the 'new in 2017' way of gating content... BOTS!

5. Talked to Your Bot. This one is exciting, but at the time of writing this book bots are fresh off the press. Who knows - if you're reading this in 2027 we may have surrendered already to the bot uprising. Facebook Messenger Bots are leading the way at the moment, and we're finding it quite exciting how we can get people to subscribe to our Facebook Messenger the same way we can our email list. You can programme your bot to answer specific questions, and release gated content to people when they ask for it - by self-serving. The best thing about this... once they've accessed this information you can jump into the conversation and talk to them 1:1.

LEAD STRENGTH

Once somebody has accessed gated content... it's now time to convince them to buy!

The first thing you need to keep in mind is 'lead strength'. Remember, we can gate a whole lot of content that shows some *potential* to buy, but the strength of that potential lead is dependent on what it is you are gating.

For example, say you have a brand-new course on 'How to de-stress your work and life to live happier'. You've built your audience, and now you want to sell this course to them.

Sales Method 1: eBook Give-Away: Create an eBook on five ways to de-stress your life. Everybody that downloads this eBook has the *potential* to buy your course, as they are clearly interested in de-stressing. However... the strength of these hand-raisers is pretty low. They may have shown potential, but you'll have to work to convert these into sales.

Sales Method 2: Waiting List: Email your whole list to tell them you are launching this course, and are only going to make it available to 20 people at a discounted rate and if they want to be added to the exclusive waiting list they need to fill out a form. Chances are you'll get a lot less uptake than the eBook, but these leads are much stronger (i.e. their hands are much higher up in the air).

One method isn't necessarily better than the other in this case, and usually it comes down to a mix, but you should keep in mind how they've raised their hand, what content they've accessed and how that relates to their lead strength!

AIDA

So now we know how strong the lead is, we need to serve content that is going to turn these leads into sales.

We've avoided using any old-fashioned marketing models up until this point, but this one lends itself perfectly to this.

Plus, we've made it a bit more relevant. So please forgive us.

Let's have a content marketing look at AIDA.

AIDA maps the different phases a person has to go through before becoming a customer of yours. It stands for:

Awareness: The person needs to be aware that your company exists
Interest: They need to be interested in what you have to offer
Desire: They need to have a desire to buy what it is you have
Action: Finally, they must take action to purchase

Can you see how this relates to Andrew and Pete's Content Model?

Awareness: Primary rich content builds awareness of your brand
Interest: Gated secondary conversion content signals interest to buy
Desire:???
Action: ???

So what about desire and action?

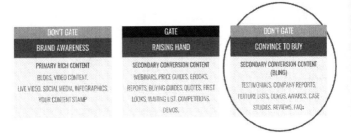

DON'T GATE	GATE	DON'T GATE
BRAND AWARENESS	RAISING HAND	CONVINCE TO BUY
PRIMARY RICH CONTENT	SECONDARY CONVERSION CONTENT	SECONDARY CONVERSION CONTENT (BLING)
BLOGS, VIDEO CONTENT, LIVE VIDEO, SOCIAL MEDIA, INFOGRAPHICS, YOUR CONTENT STAMP	WEBINARS, PRICE GUIDES, EBOOKS, REPORTS, BUYING GUIDES, QUOTES, FIRST LOOKS, WAITING LIST, COMPETITIONS, DEMOS.	TESTIMONIALS, COMPANY REPORTS, FEATURE LISTS, DEMOS, AWARDS, CASE STUDIES, REVIEWS, FAQs

Remember this?

The second type of secondary content was the 'convince to buy' content. Things like testimonials, reviews, FAQs, awards won - this type of content should be used to create the desire and action in leads, to convert them into a sale.

See how these are so much more effective at this stage of the process too?

For example, testimonials are pretty boring and irrelevant to most of your audience, but the second they are considering buying from you, hearing other people's opinions becomes a lot more interesting and relevant!

DESIRE AND ACTION

When we are looking to create **desire** in a potential customer, we should be using secondary content that convinces them that we can make their life better. We need to show the what life will be like AFTER buying from us. So use content like *testimonials, case studies and results* to paint that picture. Content like *awards and demos* are final credibility stamps to solidify that desire.

Allowing customers to take **action** is the last and final step. This is different for different businesses, but keeping the actual 'exchange of money' process as easy and straight-forward as possible is key here. If there are too many barriers in the way of a purchase, you risk losing the sale. You can also incentivise action with things like... Buy One Get One Free, Buy Now Pay Later, Free Shipping Today etc. All these sales techniques are ways of getting people over the line from lead to sale, but use with caution... they're not right in every situation!

The Higher the Desire, the Lower the Action Needed

To avoid having to focus on offers as a way to generate sales, focus on increasing the desire to buy. The higher the desire we can evoke in a lead, the less we need to focus on action.

Take Apple as an example. Every time they release a new iPhone the *desire* is sooooo huge, that their *action* is simply 'Doors are open, come and get it', and on the first day on sale... 'Doors are open, stand in a super long queue for 167,000 hours, then come and get it'.

They don't have to make the sales process any easier because the desire is so big.

What if nobody desires you?

If you are completely undesirable... well... you need a makeover!

Having a good reputation, good reviews, looking the part and having great design all helps to build desire! BUT so will your content - if you're doing it right.

Using the six previous steps of Content Mavericks, you should be whipping people up into a mad frenzy to buy from you as they are drawn into your mission, your aspirational message and your uniqueness. The more content they see of yours, the more they should be drawn in and have that desire to buy from you.

Being a *maverick* content marketer attracts people like crazy. Because you're being yourself, having fun, and doing something different - people's desire for you will increase as they want a piece of what it is you have. (*Feeling a bit hot under the collar here!*)

MAPPING OUT YOUR AIDA

Now it's time to bring all this together. We want you to map out your own AIDA.

A: What type of primary rich content are you going to create to build brand awareness, and what is your content stamp that is going to make this unique?

I: What gated secondary content do you need to create to get those all-important hand-raisers? How will you know who has potential to buy in your audience?

D: What kind of secondary content should you be creating that evokes desire to buy? How do you show somebody what life is like after buying from you?

A: How are you going to make the act of purchasing super simple? Do you need to offer any extra incentives for buying?

FISHING WITH SECONDARY CONTENT

There isn't a strict timeline for when secondary content should be offered to your audience, because the timeline is going to be different for everybody.

A customer may be convinced to take action and buy from you the same day they become aware of you, shortening the AIDA process down into a matter of hours or minutes!

Or it can literally take years for a somebody to go from the awareness stage to action.

Remember this whole process is a long-term strategy with short-term gains. The point of growing your audience and staying in touch with them with primary rich content is to build that brand equity over time, BUT if somebody is ready to buy today... you aren't turning them away!

So make sure secondary content is ALWAYS available on your website, for people to self-serve if they would like to.

Secondary Content via Email Marketing

When it comes to email marketing and keeping in touch with your audience, remember you want to get the balance right between secondary and primary content.

And the key thing here is that **it's a balance**... the more primary content you create, the more secondary content you can serve without looking like a spammer!

Your emails may look something like this then:

Week 1: Primary Rich Content
Week 2: Primary Rich Content
Week 3: Primary Rich Content
Week 4: Primary Rich Content
Week 5: Secondary Conversion Content
Week 6: Primary Rich Content

Again, there's no hard and fast rule for this, but if you do *at a minimum* three emails of primary content for every one email of secondary content you should be fine.

In this above example, anybody that raises their hand on that fifth email needs to be followed up with too remember.

You should have a content strategy in place that delivers more secondary 'convince-to-buy' content to the hand-raisers to turn them from a lead into a sale (taking them through AIDA) BUT if they don't buy at this stage, don't worry - there's always time to build more brand equity!

KEY TAKEAWAYS FROM MODULE 7: CONTENT LEAD GENERATION

The key to lead generation is creating secondary gated content that allows people to raise their hand and following up with those who are actually interested in your offering.

This way, you can be highly targeted with your sales and reduce time and resources - rather than just annoying everyone with sales messages constantly.

Mapping out your AIDA is the final step here. Remember how this ties into Andrew and Pete's Content Model to turn content into sales, in a value-adding way that doesn't come across as aggressive, desperate or sleazy.

Are you ready to become a Content Maverick?

THE END

Or is it the beginning?

Something is always 'DEAD' and something is always 'NEW'.

What you've got to be is the *MAVERICK*. Not the *MAVERICK* today, not the *MAVERICK* tomorrow, but the *MAVERICK* always.

Because *MAVERICKS* will ALWAYS stand out.

The Content Maverick doesn't do what is already being done, because they realise that they will always be one step behind the leader.

The Content Maverick is creative but organised, consistent but exciting, brings value to world but is ready to sell.

Content Marketing is vast, ever-changing, with new rules to play by and break each day.

But it's the best way to grow your business...

Best for the long term, and the short term because remember....

[let's say it together now]

> *Content Marketing is a long-term strategy that has short term gains, if executed well.*

So please, execute well.

Follow winning strategies and best practises but please don't be vanilla, don't be boring, don't do what's always been done.

Give it to your industry in a way that has never been done before. Let people fall in love with you, and let people hate you for being so bloody good.

This is the end of the book, but hopefully the beginning of something new.

Thank you so much for reading this, and we can't wait to see you breaking the internet soon.

We'll drink to that!

Andrew and Pete.

THANK YOUS

We are amazed every day how many people are nice to us. So thank you for buying this, thank you for every tweet, every email, every nice word. We love doing this kind of work, we love marketing, we love having fun, and we couldn't do it without the businesses who work with us, watch our videos, and want to listen to what we've got to say. We are super appreciative. Thank you!!!!!!!

Thank you to our amazing ATOMIC community, every single one of you. We're seeing everyone going from strength to strength, supporting each other and achieving amazing things. Your successes are down to your hard work, dedication and generally being nice people. Keep on rocking.

Friends are family - you know who you are.

And thank you to each other. That's technically a book each now! High-five! BOOM!

WANT TO HANG OUT WITH US?

ANDREWANDPETE.COM

Printed in Great Britain
by Amazon